The Way of the Lord

A NEW TESTAMENT PILGRIMAGE

Brother John
of Taizé

The Way of the Lord

A NEW TESTAMENT PILGRIMAGE

THE PASTORAL PRESS
Washington, D.C.

VERITAS PUBLICATIONS
Dublin, Ireland

ISBN 1 85390 170 9 (Veritas Publications)
ISBN 0-912405-69-4 (The Pastoral Press)

The Pastoral Press   Veritas Publications
225 Sheridan Street, NW   7/8 Lower Abbey Street
Washington, DC 20011   Dublin 1
(202) 723-1254   Ireland

The Pastoral Press is the publications division of the National Associa-
tion of Pastoral Musicians, a membership organization of musicians
and clergy dedicated to fostering the art of musical liturgy.

Printed in the United States of America

To my parents

Contents

Introduction

The following pages bring to completion an enterprise begun as a result of the "pilgrimage of reconciliation" which the Taizé Community has been undertaking, together with many others, over the past several years.

In giving Bible introductions on the topic of "faith as pilgrimage," I was led to examine this notion as a key for understanding the Judeo-Christian Scriptures. It proved to be an extremely suggestive one. The result was a book which traced out the way of the "pilgrim God" through the Hebrew Scriptures, those books that Christians improperly call the Old Testament. When I finished that work, I realized that a sequel was necessary, since with the coming of Jesus Christ the journey of faith does not come to an end but rather experiences a new beginning. The present book, therefore, is an attempt to discern the way of the Lord revealed in the life, death and resurrection of Jesus, and then in the life of the early Christians.

As I went forward with my project, its shape changed somewhat. I began with the idea of writing Bible studies on the topic of "pilgrimage" or "journey," but one after another so many captivating perspectives opened up before me that the final product resembles more closely a general introduction to the

Bible written from a particular viewpoint, that of faith as a pilgrimage or way to be followed. If the logic or rigor of the work has suffered from this, I hope that this is more than compensated for by the breadth of vision and the capacity for synthesis visible in the end result.

This book would like to offer a modest contribution to help bridge the deplorable gap between scientific exegesis on the one hand, and theology and spirituality on the other. Although it is nourished by critical and historical studies, the reflection undertaken here does not stop at a literal, archeological reading of the sacred text; it attempts to discern, beneath the letter of the writings, the footsteps of the risen Christ and the presence of his Spirit. "Even if we once knew Christ from a merely human viewpoint, we no longer know him in that way now" (2 Cor 5,16b). This book likewise takes for granted the Christological reflection of later centuries without referring to it explicitly, since it wishes above all to be a study of the New Testament on its own terms.

The notes at the end of each chapter can safely be ignored without impairing the basic argument of the book. On the other hand, it is useful to read the bible passages indicated by the references given in the text. Quotations from the New Testament are my own translations from the Greek. The Hebrew Scriptures are also cited a few times, either from the New Jerusalem Bible (NJB) or the New International Version (NIV).

For the author of these pages, it is evident that serious study and reflection have an important role to play in the understanding of Scripture. Believers cannot refuse to account for the hope that is in them (cf. 1 Peter 3,15), and a mature faith requires a level of understanding appropriate to people living in the age of computer science and microbiology. At the same time, it cannot be stressed too strongly that for believing Jews and Christians, the Bible is not a collection of ideas about God or a simple witness to Antiquity; it is a wellspring from which we can quench our thirst for God and where we can find the energy to move forward in trust. Divorced from a life of prayer, theology inevitably remains sterile; it may even suffocate us by imprisoning us in cold, lifeless systems. For people of faith, study must of necessity lead to a contemplation of the dazzling mystery of God, of the way of the Lord who crosses our path at every turn. In this fashion comprehension turns into adoration and praise,

4

and that is the only way we can deepen our relationship with the pilgrim God and follow him along life's road with all its unexpected twists and turns.

"I am the Way"

(John 14,6)

ONE

Towards the New Covenant

In a previous book[1], the theme of pilgrimage, of being-on-the-move, was used as a key for understanding the biblical message. This key proved extremely useful in helping us grasp both the essential aspects of faith and the unity of the Scriptures. Beginning with Abraham (Gen 12,1–4), the divine call turns human beings into sojourners, into pilgrims on a journey into the unknown, guided only by trust in an often elusive God. The image of the pilgrimage depicts well the open-ended character of salvation history, its creative aspect. Everything is not simply programmed ahead of time. In consenting to the call to set out on the road, believers do not give up their freedom; they acquire it to the full.

Faith is a source of freedom because it is the antithesis of a human ideology; it is not a closed system which offers ready-made answers to all human questions and problems. On the other hand, it is not mere capriciousness, nor a blind and anarchic yearning. The pilgrimage of faith is identical neither with aimless wandering nor with being comfortably settled down in the empty routines of life.

What enables us to avoid both of these pitfalls is the image of God found in Holy Scripture. The God of the Bible is not a remote divinity frozen into an immobile and inaccessible splendor. Nor is he[2] a depersonalized and uncontrollable force. He is the pilgrim God—alive, creative, resourceful. If God is the first Pilgrim, then faith consists essentially in imitating, in following, in walking in God's footsteps: it receives from God both its dynamism and its direction.

In reading the Bible, then, our primary endeavor should be to discover the footprints of the pilgrim God, to discern the way of the Lord in order to follow it. That, after all, is why those books were written in the first place. Beyond any historical or literary interest, the Bible offers us the opportunity to discover God's road so that we can make a personal decision to walk along it. An important conclusion follows from this premise: for the Jewish or Christian believer, historical investigations or literary criticism can never exhaust the meaning of a Scriptural text. Room must be given for a *spiritual* interpretation. And this interpretation can never be made solely on the basis of human rules or criteria; it is above all the fruit of a discernment that can only be received as a gift.

In the Hebrew Scriptures, our "Old Testament" that could more accurately be referred to as "the Book of the Covenant," we already encounter the notion of "the way of God." Biblical language, inevitably concrete, employs road and journey images to speak about someone's behavior, the way they live and act (PGod 46, 191ff). To take one example out of a thousand, we read that the reformer-king Josiah "walked in the ways of his father David, not turning aside to the right or to the left" (2 Chron 34,2b NIV). In consequence, the commandments are called "the ways of God" (e.g. Ps 119,3; 25,4) because they describe God's behavior, which human beings must imitate in order to be holy as God is holy (cf. Lev 19,2). The Torah or Law of God is not called the way of the Lord "only because it is commanded by him or because it leads to him, but, on a much deeper level, because it is the way he himself follows, his way in the most proper sense of the term . . . The law is the true way for man because it is the way of God." [3] For the Bible, the commandments are not arbitrary edicts of a sovereign comfortably seated on his throne but the footprints of God, a transcription of the life God leads. Believers study the Torah first of all to become familiar with the characteristics of their God, with his merciful designs, and secondly in order to imitate him, to "walk in his ways."

10

Nonetheless, the history of ancient Israel as found in the Bible is primarily the story of the nation's incapacity to find and to follow the way of God. Scripture tells us above all of God's faithfulness towards his unfaithful people, a faithfulness which obliges him to invent the most unexpected detours in order to take his partner's missteps into account. In this way the link between the Lord and his people is never completely broken, and there always exist women and men sufficiently attentive to the divine call to ensure a continuity and to permit, one day, a new beginning. For the ways of the Lord have not been written down once and for all: God is alive, and especially after the painful crisis of the Babylonian captivity, believers are longing for a brand-new intervention of the pilgrim God who will trace out his way unmistakably on the face of this earth.

The Covenant transfigured

The Book of the Covenant is thus fundamentally open-ended. The Hebrew Scriptures contain stories of the past which reveal the activity of the pilgrim God more or less clearly, and look forward to a future fulfillment. An attitude of fidelity is paramount, but this never excludes a hope resulting from trust in the living God, the inexhaustible source of Newness.

Still today, the spiritual pilgrimage of the Jewish people makes its way between these two poles of fidelity and hope, of the interpretation of the Torah and its application to the problems of the present and the future. Judaism is not, however, the only heir to the faith of Abraham, Moses and the prophets. Some two thousand years ago in Palestine, a man led in the midst of the Jewish people the life of an itinerant preacher, before being condemned, tortured and put to death by the civil and religious authorities acting in concert. His name was Jesus of Nazareth and, for some, his life represented a totally unique historical event, the transfiguration of the thousand-year-old covenant between God and humanity, in other words a fulfillment and a new starting-point.

In the eyes of his disciples, the life, the death and especially the resurrection of Jesus proved him to be the Lord and the expected Messiah (Acts 2,36). Around him a community of faith took shape, soon open not only to Jews but to believers of all

11

nations. Quickly an impressive body of literature grew up around the event, including both the story of Jesus' life and death and of the beginnings of the Christian community, and letters written to burgeoning communities in one or another city of the Mediterranean world. In this way the Christian Bible came to be made up of a "New Testament" added to the Hebrew Scriptures, from then on referred to by Christians as the "Old Testament." It is common knowledge that the word "testament" is a translation into Latin, from Greek, of the Hebrew word *"berith*, covenant"; the expression thus refers less to the books themselves than to the reality they attempt to communicate.

Given this somewhat curious composition of the Christian Bible, a question naturally arises: what is the relationship between its two parts, the two "testaments"? If the "Old Testament" is no longer valid after the coming of Jesus Christ, why continue to read and meditate on those books? If, on the other hand, the Old Testament is still essential, then why was it necessary to complete it with the New? There is nothing theoretical about these questions, as is evident from the anti-Semitic as well as the Judaizing tendencies that have influenced Christians in the course of the centuries.

Considering the biblical books primarily as written documents only complicates the question. In that case we tend to see two series of texts set over against each other, dealing largely with the same questions and thus capable of being interpreted using the same methods. It seems obvious then that we have two realities of the same order side by side, two parallel "covenants."

If, however, we start from the content, from the *significance* of the covenant between God and his people, then things take on a different appearance. It becomes clear that the two "covenants" are not on the same level. Since they are not two parallel realities of the same order, at least when they are understood on the deepest level, they cannot replace or oppose one another in an irreconcilable manner.[4]

The expression "new covenant" is found for the first time in a well-known oracle of the prophet Jeremiah, a man deeply attached to the covenant between God and the people of Israel (Jer 31,31–34). Confronted with the nation's unfaithfulness, its inability to walk in God's ways, the Lord proclaims through his prophet that he will take things into his own hands. On account of his love, in other words his compassion and his faithfulness,

12

and not because of anything his partner has done to deserve it, God will find a way to ensure that his Servant remains faithful to the end; he "will place [his] Law in the depths of their being and . . . write it on their hearts" (31,33). The new covenant is not, therefore, a new agreement similar to the old one, for in that case nothing essential would have changed. How could we be sure that human beings would be able to keep that second covenant any better than the first?

When the prophet speaks of a "new covenant," he means by it that God has committed himself to keep his relationship with his people intact come what may, by ensuring, so to speak, their fidelity as well as his own. The new covenant is thus revealed as the perfect interiorization of the covenant, the essential of the Torah fully assimilated by the human partner. Put another way, this implies the appearance of a new kind of human being, of a Servant fully able to accomplish God's will in perfect liberty. For this to be the case, it is clear that humanity as we know it would have to be transformed, and so the prophet Ezekiel with reason elaborates on Jeremiah's oracle by explaining that this new covenant will involve the presence of God's own Spirit, henceforth fully at home in the human heart (Ezek 36,27).

The disciples of Jesus discerned this "new humanity" (cf. Eph 2,15) in the person of their Master, especially in the light of his resurrection from the dead. They saw him as the perfect human being because he was God's presence in the midst of humanity, and in that way the fulfillment of the covenant, or more exactly the covenant made flesh. In Jesus, God walks along our roads in human form, and so the way of God is fully traced out in human history by one like us.[5] If Jesus Christ is God's definitive "Yes" to his creation and to his people, he is at the same time (and as a result) humanity's "Yes" to God (cf. 2 Cor 1,17–22). He is the Servant of the Lord *par excellence* (Matt 12,15–21), the man who possesses the Holy Spirit "without limit" (John 3,34).

If in Jesus the "new covenant" or the covenant brought to fulfillment takes shape, then it seems to follow naturally that in him the history of salvation has reached its end. A comprehensible perspective, shared to some extent by the first generations of Christians who made frequent use of eschatological categories of thought to interpret the Event of Christ: by his coming "the last days" have begun (Heb 1,2; Acts 2,17; 1 Peter 1,20). And yet history goes on, the fulfillment of the covenant shows itself to be not an ending but rather a new starting-point. The "end of the age" is shown to be not a chronological period of time but a new, life-giving Presence discernible beneath the surface of the old eon, a leaven of renewal at work in the dough of our dying world. For it is not enough that one individual live in perfect fidelity to God; the one who receives the fullness of the Spirit must be the same one who gives it to his fellows (John 1,33; 3,34; 7,37–39) so that he can be "the firstborn of many brothers and sisters" (Rom 8,29). As the centuries pass, the Risen Christ continues to call men and women to follow him, so that in the end the covenant may lead to a blessing offered to all people transformed into a single human family (cf. Gen 12,3).

"I am the Way"

After this brief sketch of the logic of the covenant between God and his people transmitted by the Scriptures, let us take up the relationship between the two parts of our Bible from another point of view. One of the first names given to Christians, according to the Acts of the Apostles, was "followers of the Way" (Acts 9,2). In the Book of Acts, we find expressions like "the Way of the Lord" (18,25), "the Way of salvation" (16,17) and especially "the Way," with no qualifications (9,2; 18,26; 19,9.23; 22,4; 24,14.22), used to describe the life lived by those who follow faithfully in the footsteps of Jesus Christ.[6] In the consciousness of the early Christians, then, Christianity was not a new religion or sect but essentially a *way*, a way of life. Even more, it was not just one way among others but *the* Way, the pilgrim God's own path. From now on, in their thinking, the way of the Lord was not revealed simply by external commandments, by a Torah that had to be interpreted and assimilated; this Way had taken human form and was present and active in the midst of human life. By sending his own Son, God traced for us "a new and living way" (Heb 10,20), his own Way, in the midst of human history.

In the Gospel according to John, Jesus sums up this understanding in a few words spoken to his disciples who want to be shown the Father and to understand their Teacher's secret: "I am the Way" (John 14,6). He then goes on to say, "Whoever has

14

seen me has seen the Father" (14,9).[7] Jesus reveals God's will fully by living it out. Following him, therefore, means choosing to walk along that Way in the concrete conditions of our own existence. By our life as pilgrims in the steps of Christ, we are called to make present for a particular time and place the way of the Lord. As Saint Paul expresses it, "It is no longer I who live; it is Christ living in me" (Gal 2,20).

We have already seen how, in the Hebrew Scriptures, the path of the pilgrim God takes shape little by little in the history of the people of Israel. This path had to be discerned; it was not fully accessible even to those who were in the process of living it out, in a manner analogous to the way we are not ourselves aware of the full significance of the lives we are living. This is because faith, by its nature, is open-ended; it involves a setting out into the unknown (PGod 17–22, 111). Now this path, the footprints of the pilgrim God, is in fact the Gospel of Jesus Christ, not as a collection of books, a text added to the "Old Testament," but as the Risen Christ himself who continues his journey from death to Life in the existence of the community of believers. The Gospel is thus not, in the deepest sense, something that comes *after* the Book of the Covenant but something *within* it. It is its deepest meaning, what it is really about, the key that can unlock its secrets. Or, to use a more biblical expression, it is its *recapitulation* (cf. Eph 1,10).

The first generations of Christians grasped this truth by a kind of instinct. When confronted by their so-called allegorical or spiritual exegesis, ready to discover the presence of Christ everywhere in the ancient Scriptures, the modern reader is generally somewhat ill-at-ease. But despite the inevitable excesses in practice, the basic intuition of their method remains valuable and revelant for us today. "*Spiritalis intelligentia in Veteri Testamento, nihil est aliud quam Novum Testamentum* (Spiritual understanding in the Old Testament is nothing other than the New Testament)."[8] Or as Saint Augustine put it in a much-quoted and more condensed saying: "*In Vetere Novum latet et in Novo Vetus patet* (in the Old [Testament] the New lies hidden and in the New the Old finds expression)."[9] In the language of this book we can express it thus: the way of God which can be detected in the Scriptures of the people of Israel is nothing other than the hidden presence of Christ the Pilgrim (cf. 1 Cor 10,4; John 8,56). If this is the case, then it is impossible to be satisfied with a

15

purely historical, exterior interpretation of biblical realities. Although this has its place, limiting ourselves to such a reading would mean neglecting the deepest meaning of these realities. It would mean reducing the Word of God to a letter that kills rather than finding in it a source of Life (cf. 2 Cor 3,6).

Between "the Law and the prophets" on the one hand, and the presence of Christ in the life of the Christian community on the other, are found the books of the New Testament. What is their place in the framework we have just sketched out?[10] It should now be clear that as written documents, they are not in themselves, strictly speaking, the new covenant or the Gospel. First of all, these texts communicate to us the Event that marks the fulfillment of the covenant, in other words the appearance on the stage of history of the new covenant: the life of Jesus, and above all his "passover" from death to eternity's life resulting in the gift of the Holy Spirit and the creation of the Church. These writings thus enable us to enter into contact with the paschal Christ and, by an act of faith, to set out in his footsteps. In the second place, the books of the New Testament are a spiritual commentary on the Scriptures in the light of the resurrection of Jesus Christ. They attempt to show just how the Event of Christ provides the key to understand a historical process which until then had remained more or less enigmatic and incomplete; they indicate in what way he is the recapitulation of that process (cf. Luke 24,27.45).

The four gospels, which basically tell the story of Jesus' earthly life, require an even more nuanced evaluation. The events of Jesus' life before the resurrection belong to both the old and the new economy of salvation*: the seed has now appeared in the world, but it has not yet fallen into the earth to die and bear fruit (cf. John 12,24). To discover their full significance, these events must be read in the light of what follows, the death and resurrection of Christ, and in that sense they resemble the events narrated in the Hebrew Scriptures. On the other hand, it is no less true that Jesus' life forms a unity: from the very first moment of

---

*The word "economy" comes from the Greek word *oikonomia*, the art of administering a household. It refers to the fact that the will of God is accomplished by stages in human history. Like a good administrator or educator, God prepares his people little by little to enter into the fullness of his communion.

his existence he accomplishes the will of God fully; he runs unswervingly along the Way (cf. Heb 10,5–7).

Four approaches to the Gospel

In the prologue to his gospel, each evangelist reflects in his own way on the theme that concerns us here, the relationship between the history of the chosen people and "the Good News of Jesus Christ" (Mark 1,1). Let us examine one after another their different but converging outlooks.

The prologue of MARK (1,1–13) is centered on the figure of John the Baptist and his relationship to Jesus. John, the preacher of a return to the Lord in order to receive forgiveness, a desert-dweller clothed like Elijah (1,6; 2 Kings 1,8), is the fine flower of the religion of Israel. A worthy successor to the prophets, he calls the inhabitants of Judea and Jerusalem out into the wilderness, the most appropriate place since the long-ago days of the Exodus for a preparation, a new beginning. And he proclaims the coming of "someone more powerful" who will inaugurate the last days by pouring forth God's Holy Spirit. Surprisingly and unexpectedly, this person who comes later in reality occupies the first place; the Baptizer is worthy only to be his slave. Instead of following in John's footsteps, the newcomer will lead the way.

To justify the mission of John, Mark begins his gospel with an amalgam of biblical quotations centered on the theme of "the way" drawn from the Book of Exodus and the prophets Malachi and Second Isaiah. In themselves, these texts refer to the road in the wilderness along which God led the Israelites during the Exodus (Ex 23,20), to God's return to Palestine with the former captives after the Exile (Isa 40,3), and finally to the coming of the Lord at the end of time to purify the Temple (Mal 3,1). But for Mark, this "way of the Lord" prepared by John, the road which in the ancient Scriptures is that taken by the nation but still more by God, is in fact the way of Christ. The pilgrimage undertaken by Jesus and prepared by John, the Good News of Jesus Christ that is now beginning, has been traced out for a long time already, and so John is right when he senses that in Jesus, the more powerful one, he encounters the one who goes before him (cf. John 1,15.30).

17

At the center of Mark's prologue we find the encounter between John and Jesus. Apparently it is for a baptism, an act of purification, but it resembles more closely a transmission of powers, as during the anointing of Saul, the first king of Israel, by Samuel, the last of the judges (1 Sam 10). With this act John's role is over and he disappears from the scene. Jesus is led by God's Spirit into the desert to confront the forces of evil, and the prologue concludes with a quick glimpse of creation reconciled, a return to paradise: Man in the center surrounded by the angels and the beasts.

Mark indicates in yet another way the link between Jesus and the tradition from which he comes. The Baptist's presence and Jesus' willingness to be baptized shows his profound continuity with the religion of his people, with their history as sinners constantly in need of God's forgiveness (cf. Matt 3,14–15). But at the very moment when he consents to the requirements of the past something new and unexpected happens; there is a sudden and direct revelation of God, and John fades into the background. Jesus' baptism becomes the occasion for an encounter between heaven and earth, for a brand-new sending of the Creator Spirit, for a definitive revelation of God's loving designs made concrete in the person of his "beloved Son." The preparation was essential and salutary, but when the time of fulfillment arrives it resembles a shadow as compared to the reality. Or to express it more exactly, everything valuable it contained is seen to be already a part of the final result, bathed in its luminosity, like the first rays of the dawn before the sun when it finally rises.

The two other synoptic* gospels likewise examine the relation between the covenant with Israel and the Event of Jesus Christ. They do it by taking up different traditions surrounding the birth of Jesus. MATTHEW 1–2 begins with a genealogy, a profoundly biblical manner of indicating someone's rootedness in a history. Humanly speaking, Jesus is thus shown to be a descendant of David and of Abraham (Matt 1,1), in other words the expected Messiah and the heir to the Promise. In addition to this regular succession of generations there is, however, another side, unex-

---

*The gospels of Matthew, Mark and Luke are known collectively as the *synoptic* gospels on account of their similarities of structure and content. They can be set side by side in parallel columns and thus taken in at a single glance.

18

pected and irregular, linked to the direct action of the Holy Spirit and symbolized by the presence of women in the genealogy. At the end (1,16) these two aspects are both brought to a climax: after centuries of preparation all at once the chain is broken, and Mary remains alone in her vulnerability which is at the same time openness to the divine Spirit, a new beginning.

The following paragraph (1,18–25) expresses the same thing in story form. The unexpected is represented by Mary, who is "with child by the Holy Spirit" (1,18). But the incarnation is incomplete until the child receives a name and a patrimony. This is the role of Joseph, the "righteous man" (1,19) who must take care of "the child and his mother" while remaining in the background.

Matthew is especially interested in the figure of Joseph, a man of the covenant who becomes a man of the Gospel by his trust and his consequent willingness to respond to demands that remain incomprehensible to him. Righteous like Abraham ready to give back to God what is dearest to his heart, his only son (Gen 22), righteous like the Baptist willing to become less so that Christ can be more (John 3,30), Joseph is also an image of the believer who is happy to give his life rather than to cling to it (cf. Mark 8,34–37). In him the Law shades imperceptibly into the Gospel; covenant and new covenant coincide.

Joseph's readiness to allow himself to be led by God often places the holy family on the road. The child Jesus personally accomplishes the thousand-year-long pilgrimage of his people. He goes down to Egypt like the patriarchs and returns like the Israelites led by Moses. The evangelist thus uses the means at his disposal to state, in his own way, the thesis of this chapter: Jesus recapitulates in himself the history of his people; the way of the Lord traced out in the Scriptures is in fact the way of Christ.

In Matthew's prologue we likewise find the opposite movement, the movement of others *toward* Jesus. In the story of the coming of the wise men (2,1–12), the evangelist sees a sign that the prophetic oracles concerning the pilgrimage of the nations up to the holy City at the end of time are approaching their fulfillment (e.g. Isa 2,1–5; 60,1ff; cf. PGod 124–127, 154–155). Nevertheless Jerusalem, where King Herod reigns by violence, is eclipsed by the small town of Bethlehem, birthplace of the Messiah-king Jesus. The malevolent power of Herod causes pain and suffering (2,16–18) but is unable to counteract the plan of God (cf. 27,62ff, the guards at the tomb). Bethlehem, where King David was born long ago, symbolizes both continuity and a new beginning, a return to the roots in order to set out again. The new departure is both a fulfillment of past expectations and a reversal of human values.

LUKE 1 sums up the entire history of salvation by telling the story of two families. John's parents are righteous and blameless but sterile (Luke 1,6–7); they are thus worthy successors of Abraham and Sarah. Zechariah, a man of the Temple, receives word of God's entry into the world but his trust is not complete. As a result he is struck dumb and thus cannot pronounce God's blessing that normally marks the conclusion of the liturgy (1,22). That blessing will have to take a long detour, and even pass through death before it reaches its destination (2,34; 24,50).

To make a new step forward possible, the family of Jesus has to take over. Luke for his part is especially interested in the figure of Mary, the mother of Jesus. In his eyes, she recapitulates the best of the spiritual history of Israel, and that is perhaps the reason why he describes her using a whole series of biblical allusions. Daughter Zion ready to greet her Savior in joy (1,28; Zeph 3,14–18; Zech 2, 14(10); 9,9–10), Ark of the Covenant travelling in the hill country (1,39–45; 2 Sam 6), by her yes spoken in trust Mary enables God to enter into history in a brand-new and definitive fashion. In her, God chooses from among his people what is apparently of small worth in human eyes so that his free and undeserved gift of love may shine out more clearly in all its splendor (1,46–55; cf. 1 Cor 1,18–29).

Through this story of two families, Luke describes the relationship between God and his people as one of both continuity and the unexpected, of fidelity that has to pass through a kind of death and resurrection. To become fully itself, the covenant has to set out on roads never before travelled. When Elizabeth recognizes in Mary the mother of her Lord who is coming to her (1,43), she ratifies this reversal of values and allows an inexhaustible flood of praise to well up to God from the depths of his creation.

The second chapter of Luke's gospel consists in a journey back and forth between faraway Galilee and Judea, the center of the nation. Mary and Joseph travel to Bethlehem in apparent obedience to the emperor's edict, but on a deeper level to allow the

Messiah to be born in "the city of David." Later on, Jesus' parents bring the newborn infant to the Temple to fulfill "everything according to the Law of the Lord" (2,39) and, when he is twelve years old, we see Jesus at home in the Temple disputing with the teachers of the Law. The Jewishness of Jesus, his conformity to the religion of his ancestors, is thus emphasized, as well as the element of newness, of fulfillment, since the ancient prophecies concerning the Lord's entry into his sanctuary (Mal 3) are now in the process of realization.

The first people to witness this fulfillment are "God's poor," the faithful remnant of the nation: the shepherds (2,8ff), Mary herself who "retained all these things, pondering them in her heart" (2,19.51), and finally, Simeon and Anna. These two old people are presented as the best of Israel, and the "now" spoken by Simeon the Righteous (2,29–32) symbolizes the passing of the former economy of salvation and the beginning of a time when salvation is explicitly open to all; waiting (2,25) is changed into seeing with one's own eyes (2,30). Nonetheless, the shadow of the cross is not absent from these chapters (2,7.34–35.48), as if to warn us right from the start that the time of fulfillment will not come without passing through a trial, without "a fall and a rise." For Luke, the coming of Christ is, in a word, the *fulfillment* of the covenant, that is, it reveals the full meaning of past events and responds to longings and expectations, though in an unpredictable way that does not exclude incomprehension and suffering, a *trial* in the deepest sense of the word.

JOHN, in his inimitable fashion, expresses the same thing from a much more universal perspective. In the prologue to his gospel (John 1,1–18), he does not only situate Jesus with respect to Israel; he depicts all of creation and history in its relationship with God. This relationship is the work of the one John names the *Logos*, the Word of God, and whom he considers as a subject distinct from God while at the same time being one with him. In the course of the prologue, the relation between the Word and the world becomes clearer and clearer, like a camera lens that becomes ever more sharply focussed. The Word of God is presented as the means of creation and a source of illumination of every human being (1,1–9a). It comes into the world and comes to its own people (1,9b-11), without being recognized or welcomed adequately. Finally the evangelist tells us that the Word, present from the beginning, takes on human form and

21

becomes one of us: "The Word was made flesh and dwelt among us" (1,14a). The synthetic outlook of John includes the perspective of the other gospels while going much further. In God's plan the covenant with Israel ("his own," 1,11) is the climax of a series of attempts by which God tries to illuminate and direct his creation. Even if none of these efforts are fully successful, God does not abandon the world for all that. He goes further and further in his attempt to make himself understood and in the end enters visibly, as one human being among others, in the world he created and in the midst of his people. The birth of Jesus is thus revealed as the perfect expression, in human history, of God's basic intention from the very beginning, namely, to bring humanity into communion with himself or, to use John's own language, to enable us to become children of God (1,12). And John, like the other evangelists, situates the Baptist with respect to the coming of Christ: the precursor comes to bear witness to the light (1,7), and he knows that in fact Jesus is before him (1,15). Here too, the last are in fact the first.

John expresses the relationship between Jesus and the covenant of Sinai in another way as well:

For the Law was given through Moses;
grace and truth came through Jesus Christ. (1,17)

It is essential to understand that, in this verse, the gift of the Law is in no way underrated or derided by the evangelist. Blinded by a too facile opposition resulting from a superficial reading of Saint Paul, we are tempted to consider the pair Law—Gospel as the equivalent of the pair darkness—light. Here, such an interpretation would be quite clearly incorrect. The relation is rather that indicated in the preceding verse, *charin anti charitos*, "grace for grace" (1,16), in other words a free gift replaced by another reality of the same order.[11]

What is, more exactly, the progression here? What relationship is there between the Law on the one hand and "grace and truth" on the other? In Judaism, the Law is often set in parallel to the truth, because it reveals the will of God, his Way. At the same time, the notion of the truth is wider than that of the Law. We can say that it designates the content or the significance of the Law for believers. It refers to God's designs revealed, his "secret" told. According to Saint John, then, in the life of Jesus

22

Christ the fundamental content of the Torah, its truest significance, is fully accessible to us. The way of the Lord, hidden beneath the surface of the Scriptures, becomes a human life. The outer covering breaks open and the fruit becomes visible. *In Vetere Novum latet et in Novo Vetus patet.*[12]

The relationship we have just examined between the way of the Lord and the Event of Jesus Christ provides the structure for the following chapters. In these pages, we will attempt first to discover the pilgrimage undertaken by Jesus during his earthly life and transmitted by the four gospels, the journey of a man among men which is also the way of the Lord. This attempt is quite similar to the one made in studying Israel's history in a previous book. With the difference, however, that here we shall be particularly attentive to the life of Jesus as a *recapitulation* of the ancient Scriptures: on the one hand, the true significance of this life is only clear on the basis of the history that leads up to it, and on the other, this life alone, in the eyes of Christians, sheds full light on a history which otherwise remains in part enigmatic and obscure. In reading the gospels, we shall thus attempt to understand Jesus against the background of the centuries-old tradition of his people.

Subsequently, following the order of the books of the New Testament, we will see the way of Christ become the way of Christians, as the Risen Lord continues on his road in the life of the community of believers. Although they take the pilgrimage of Jesus, notably his journey from death to life, as a source and a permanent model for the life of faith, the apostolic letters are turned primarily towards the present, towards the often arduous attempt to follow this road in the circumstances of daily life. The future likewise remains significant; for the followers of Christ, it implies the definitive and glorious manifestation of what they are already living out in a hidden way amidst the trials and uncertainties of the present. In this way the new covenant goes beyond the writings of the first Christians. The way of the Lord leaves the pages of the Book to become the pilgrimage of every man or woman who is ready to risk his or her life for the sake of Christ and the Gospel.

Questions for Reflection

1. Biblical faith is neither an infringement on human freedom nor an incitement to spiritual anarchy but an invitation to set out in the footsteps of the pilgrim God. What consequences does this statement have for my own life?

2. In what way does the life of Jesus make concrete the oracle of the prophet Jeremiah concerning a "new covenant" (Jer 31,31–34)? How does the Christian life fulfill this prophecy?

3. In the Hebrew Scriptures, little by little the pilgrim God reveals his way to the people of Israel. Now Jesus tells us, "I am the Way" (John 14,6). What should a Christian's attitude be toward the sacred books of Israel, our "Old Testament"? How should a disciple of Christ read and understand those books?

4. The prologues of the four gospels (Mark 1,1–13; Matt 1–2; Luke 1–2; John 1,1–18) situate Jesus in the context of salvation history. What can we learn from these texts about Jesus? What do they tell us in particular about the relation between Jesus and God's activity throughout the centuries to bring human beings to the fullness of life?

Notes

[1]*The Pilgrim God: A Biblical Journey,* (Washington D.C.: The Pastoral Press, 1985), henceforth referred to in the text as PGod followed by the page numbers.

[2]Following the practice of Scripture and to avoid linguistic acrobatics, I use masculine pronouns to refer to God when necessary. For a fuller discussion see PGod 25, note 1.

[3]Stanislas Lyonnet, " 'La Voie' dans les Actes des Apôtres," *Recherches de Science Religieuse* 69, 1981–1, p. 157.

[4]If we consider the Sinai covenant as an agreement between two partners founded upon a list of duties, it can be said that after the coming of Christ this covenant lost its validity for Christians, in the sense that they are no longer required to fulfill all the precepts of the Jewish Law in order to ensure their communion with God. This is the perspective of Saint Paul in some of his letters, when he is faced with people who have not understood the new situation brought about by the coming of Jesus Christ (e.g. Gal 2,16; Rom 7,1–6). On the other hand, Paul constantly attempts to root the gospel message in the spiritual history of his people by going back to Abraham and by emphasizing the no-

tions of *faith* and *promise* present from the very beginning of the history of God's people (Gal 3,6ff; Rom 4). Spiritually, Christians are sons and daughters of Abraham (Gal 4,21–31). Moreover, for Paul the Law is holy and righteous and good (Rom 7,12); it comes from the Spirit (Rom 7,14); it leads to Christ (Gal 3,24; Rom 10,4). The apostle understands the events surrounding the life and death of Jesus in terms of the power of evil obscuring the true purpose of the Law, namely to point to true Life, and turning it into an instrument of death, of spiritual pride (Rom 7,7–13). It is thus the Law turned into a caricature of itself that is opposed to the Gospel, in other words the covenant reduced to its outward aspects and preferred to faith in Christ. The new covenant is thus, once again, the covenant renewed. By living lives of selfless love, the disciples of Christ do the essential of what the Torah requires (Rom 13,8–10; Gal 5,14). Strictly speaking, it is more exact to speak of two economies of salvation than of two covenants.

[5]Cf. Pope John Paul II, Encyclical letter *Redemptor hominis* (March 4, 1979), no. 13: "Jesus Christ is the chief way for the Church. He Himself is our way 'to the Father's house' (cf. John 14,1f) and is the way to each man." And in this context the pope takes up the words of Vatican II: "By His Incarnation, He, the Son of God, in a certain way united himself with each man" (*Ibid.*).

[6]For this topic see the enlightening article of the late Father Lyonnet quoted above, note 3.

[7]For an interpretation of these verses see Ignace de la Potterie, *La Vérité dans saint Jean. Tome I: Le Christ et la vérité, l'Esprit et la vérité* (Analecta Biblica, 73) (Rome: Biblical Institute Press, 1977), pp. 241–278. Christ is the Way *because* he is the Truth (his existence reveals fully the Father's designs) and the Life (he already bestows on believers God's own Life). He can be the Way because he is both the Word of Life turned toward God (John 1,1–2; 1 John 1,2) and fully in solidarity with creation ("the flesh," John 1,14).

[8]The quotation is from a Latin Church father (Berengaudus) and taken from Henri de Lubac, *The Sources of Revelation* (New York: Herder & Herder, 1968), p. 122. The masterly studies of Cardinal de Lubac on the allegorical exegesis of Origen and the Middle Ages are not merely of historical interest. They present a theological truth of the first order concerning the interpretation of the Scriptures that we neglect today at our own peril.

[9]*Quaestiones in Heptateucheum*, 2, 73 (PL 34, 623), quoted in Vatican II, *Constitution on Divine Revelation ("Dei Verbum")*, no. 16.

[10]See De Lubac, pp. 194–217.

[11]See De la Potterie, pp. 142–150.

[12]This interpretation of the progression in John 1,17 is in harmony with the reading of Ignace de la Potterie (*op. cit.*, pp. 117–241) that translates

"grace and truth" by "the free gift of the truth." It is also compatible with the interpretation that sees these words as a translation of the Hebrew *hesed we'emeth* ("loving-kindness and faithfulness," Ex 34,6; Ps 86,15), the basic characteristics of the God of the covenant. Cf. Andre Feuillet, *Le Prologue du quatrième évangile. Etude de théologie johannique* (Paris: Desclée de Brouwer, 1968), pp. 114–115. In both cases there is a progression from an external reality to its inner meaning, from an envelope to its contents.

TWO

Synoptics I, The Paths of the Kingdom

It is certainly not by chance that the very structure of the gospels is commanded by the notion of pilgrimage, that they essentially describe a journey, a path. For Mark, followed in this by Matthew and Luke, the public life of Jesus takes place in two stages: first, an itinerant ministry in the towns and countrysides of Galilee, then a journey up to Jerusalem, the place of his death and resurrection. According to Scripture scholars, in all probability this framework is more theological than historical. We know from John's gospel that Jesus visited the Holy City several times in the course of his life, and this seems more plausible from a purely historical point of view. The two stages of the synoptic gospels thus appear to characterize the theological contours of the pilgrimage of Jesus. This is what we are now going to attempt to lay out, relying principally on the gospel of Mark, then completing our discoveries by the witnesses of Matthew and Luke.

The One-who-comes

First and foremost there is a simple and obvious fact to which attention should be drawn: the gospels describe nothing other than the movements of a man who never stays in one place. The life of Jesus is a life on the road. Jesus deserves the title of Pilgrim first of all because of this itinerant existence of his. He has no place to lay his head (Luke 9,58), and he spends his time going from one village to another in Palestine (Mark 6,6). But this apparently simple fact is in reality of great significance: Jesus is not the Pilgrim in externals alone; his life on the road is the key to his real identity, a language used by God to communicate the mystery of his being and his love.

In two verses with which Mark summarizes the beginning of Jesus' ministry, we begin already to glimpse the true meaning of his identity as a wayfarer:

> After John had been handed over, Jesus came to Galilee pro-
> claiming the Good News of God and saying, "The time of fulfill-
> ment has come and the Reign of God is at hand; change your
> hearts and believe in the Good News!" (Mark 1,14–15)

The end of the activity of John, last and greatest of the proph-ets of the covenant (cf. Matt 11,7–15), marks the end of an era. Something brand-new is in the air, a new beginning that is at the same time a fulfillment of past longings. To describe this new beginning, Mark employs a seemingly ordinary verb but one that in fact reveals the heart of the biblical message: Jesus *came. . .*

This verb "to come" recalls at once all the interventions of God in the course of salvation history. In the oldest layers of the Bible, the God of Israel is acclaimed as the God-who-comes, who breaks into human history to do battle on behalf of his people (Deut 33,2; Judg 5,4; Ps 18,9; 68,7.17; cf. PGod 30f, 173). This language is taken up by the prophets (Isa 30,27; 40,10; Micah 1,3; Hab 3,3) and is employed after the Exile in the "proto-apocalyptic" literature (Isa 59,19–20; 63,1; 66,15; 35,4; Zech 14,5; Ps 50,3) to confess faith in a God who is actively concerned about his chosen ones, who will take action to save them from their enemies. In the Bible, God is first and foremost the one who comes. A very few texts, often enigmatic, apply the expression to a figure distinct from God (Zech 9,9; Dan 7,13; Ps 118,26; Gen 49,10?), but the person in question is always considered from the side of God, so to speak, as someone sent by God or some-one who is overshadowed by God.

30

Even before the editorial usage of the verb "to come" by the gospel writers, we find it on the lips of Jesus himself. Here we have an important and often neglected fact to help us approach the self-understanding of someone who almost never shares with us an introspective self-analysis. "I did not come to call the righteous, but sinners ... I did not come to bring peace, but a sword ... I have come to cast fire on the earth" (Mark 2,17; Matt 10,34; Luke 12,49). And sometimes, identifying himself with the Son of Man, an eschatological figure who comes in the visions of the Book of Daniel: "The Son of Man did not come to be served but to serve, and to give his life as a ransom for the multitude ... The Son of Man came to seek and to save what was lost" (Mark 10,45; Luke 19,10). In the very depths of his being, Jesus is possessed by the awareness that he is acting in place of the pilgrim God; he is the One-who-comes.

As the centuries passed, the hoped-for coming of the pilgrim God (or of his representative) tended to take on an *eschatological* significance for the People of God, that it, it came to signify the end of the present age and the dawn of a brand-new era. And so, when he describes the beginning of Jesus' activity as a coming (1,7.9.14), Mark very discreetly tells us that this turning-point in human history is now taking place. The following words emphasize the reason for this coming: Jesus comes to the land of Israel "proclaiming the Good News of God." This phrase evokes another announcement made some five centuries earlier by an anonymous prophet at the time when the Babylonian captivity was drawing to an end:

> How beautiful on the mountains
> are the feet of those who bring good news,
> who proclaim peace,
> who bring good tidings,
> who say to Zion,
> "Your God reigns!" (Isa 52,7 NIV)[1]

Putting these texts side by side helps us see two things more clearly. First of all, the "good news" in question does not refer to a small personal happiness but is the announcement of an earth-shattering event: God is entering into the world as a liberating presence to annul the consequences of evil and to offer his people a new life.[2] Secondly, the bearer of the good news (in

31

Greek, the "evangelist") is part and parcel of the fulfillment he announces. His footsteps on the hills of Judah are a first sign of the new springtime that is beginning. Since God brings about this transformation of history by means of his word, a comprehension of the event is inseparable from the event itself. It cannot be understood from without. The herald is not a forerunner like the meteorologist who announces the coming of spring; he resembles instead the first buds that appear on the trees.

The terms of the proclamation reinforce this link between the message and the messenger. First of all, by means of two verbs in the perfect tense, we hear an announcement of the new situation that is beginning: "The time of fulfillment has come and the Kingdom of God is at hand." The perfect tense in Greek indicates the present state of affairs resulting from a past activity; it is thus a way of emphasizing both the present and past dimensions of the new reality. There is an accent on the here-and-now, and yet what happens today is somehow the culmination of an ongoing process. In these phrases there is both the "already present" and the "not yet," or more accurately the "constantly in the process of coming." The time of fulfillment (*kairos*) has now arrived, but it will never be over and done with. The word *kairos,* incidentally, is never used to mean a duration, the kind of time that flows; it refers to a specific moment when something happens. Likewise the Kingdom, Rule or Reign of God, for which the faithful have been longing for centuries now, has come close and is presently in a state of permanent closeness. The phrase could thus be translated, "is near," "is at hand" or even, less accurately, "has come."

With these very simple means at his disposal, Mark wants to help us understand right from the start the paradoxical dynamics of the Gospel, a paradox that results when the Absolute of God breaks into human history. Humanly speaking, how could we explain a "time" that does not pass but that always remains crouched at the door like a lion ready to spring, or a "kingdom" that is always coming, that is present insofar as it is on its way and is on its way insofar as it is present? In any case, it is this humanly inexplicable reality that makes possible and necessary the rest of the proclamation. Two imperatives indicate the human response to God's utterly free gift: change your hearts and believe! To enter into the new reality that is coming, there is no other road but an act of trust and a change of outlook[3] that must be continually renewed (the present imperative in Greek has the force of an imperfect or continuous tense; it expresses a repeated activity, not a once-and-for-all act). We cannot grasp what is happening while remaining on the outside; the only way to understand is to open ourselves to a transformation of our whole being, by running over and over again the risk of faith.

The beginning of Jesus' public life in Mark's gospel thus forms a remarkable parallel with the origins of the people of God in chapter 12 of the Book of Genesis (Gen 12,1–4; PGod ch. 1). We are in the presence of the same logic of a free gift of new life that leads to a break with the past, to a radical change of life-style. The parallel becomes even more evident in the next section (Mark 1,16–20), the call of the first disciples. They are asked to leave everything behind in order to set out on the road with Jesus. With respect to the call of Abraham there is a similar structure but a different emphasis: here the fulfillment is more important than the promise, and in place of the invisible pilgrim-God there is the man Jesus, a human being like us who nonetheless "comes" just like the Kingdom he proclaims.

Words of life and acts of healing

This coming of Jesus is spelled out in the following chapters; the key aspects of his activity in Galilee are presented using concrete examples. First of all by a "typical" day in the lakeside town of Capernaum. Jesus enters the town and comes to the synagogue to teach (1,21). There is nothing theoretical or conventional about his teaching, however. It possesses an astonishing power that can leave people dumbfounded (1,22) and even triumph over the spirits of evil (1,23–26). Like the God of Israel seen by Isaiah (e.g. Isa 1,4; 6,3), Jesus is the Holy One whose simple presence unmasks and banishes the forces of evil. Significantly, his adversary has no illusions as to the significance of the event: "What do you want with us, Jesus of Nazareth? Have you come to destroy us? I know who you are: the Holy One of God" (1,24).

Coming from the synagogue, Jesus then comes into Simon's house. He comes to Simon's mother-in-law, sick in bed, and "raises her up." The act of healing is an admirable illustration of the mission of Jesus. His coming inspires fear and apprehension in evil spirits but brings a fullness of life to human beings in need (and who is not?). Not for nothing does the last scene of the day show Jesus healing "the whole town" (1,32–34); the salvation he brings, even at its humble beginnings, already contains a seed of universality.

This widening of perspectives continues in the following verses (1,35–39). After such a day filled with encounters, Jesus leaves the town very early in the morning and comes to a lonely place. He does this in order to renew his intimacy with God, but also to widen the scope of his ministry: "Let us go elsewhere, into the surrounding regions, so that I can proclaim the message there as well, for that is why I have come out" (1,38). The Good News cannot be limited to the needs of a single town . . . or a single nation.

The entire first section of the gospel according to Mark (1,14—8,26) is structured as a journey through the region of Galilee, with a few brief excursions into neighboring areas. Jesus comes to towns and villages, sometimes entering the local synagogue (3,1; 6,2) or staying in a house (2,1.15; 3,20). He goes through fields (2,23) and often walks alongside the lake of Galilee (2,13; 3,7; 4,1) or crosses it in a boat (4,35ff; 5,21; 6,45ff; 8,10). Once, before making an important decision, he even goes up into the hills (3,13). His activity consists in the proclamation of the Good News of salvation, in words and in deeds. Often he explains his message by borrowing images and comparisons from everyday life, the parables (ch. 4), and makes it concrete by acts of healing, in a confrontation with the forces of evil.

For Jesus, however, the act of healing sick bodies is only the sign of a deeper and more radical healing. Its name is "the forgiveness of sins." We see this in the story of his encounter with a paralyzed man (2,1–12). Four stretcher-bearers are necessary to bring this man, frozen into immobility, to Jesus and, instead of the expected words of healing, Jesus merely says, "My child, your sins are forgiven" (2,5). The hearers are taken aback. Jesus then continues by healing the man's body, and this act thus becomes the sign of a new life that transforms the being down to its very depths, bringing an astonishing new lightness and dynamism. Rise up and walk! Forgiveness removes the burdens of the past, and turns a person paralyzed by past mistakes into a pilgrim walking, with lightened step, along the way of the Lord.

The coming of Jesus, envoy of the pilgrim God, perturbs the ordinary course of events; it sets up an almost spontaneous movement by which others "come" in their turn. The news is passed from one person to the next with the force of an electric current. After the first act of healing accomplished by Jesus in Mark's gospel, the evangelist explains that "his reputation (*akoē*) immediately spread everywhere" (1,28). We would do well not to separate this renown from the content of the message itself, but see it rather as its "echo" in the ears and in the lives of the listeners, themselves transformed into pilgrims travelling on the road. Thus we read immediately afterwards that "the whole town was gathered before the door" (1,33) and, a little later, "people kept coming to him from everywhere" (1,45b; cf. 3,20).

This spread of the Good News seems to occur as well when its bearer is unaware of it, or even consciously opposed. Here we encounter the well-known theme of the "messianic secret" discovered generations ago in the gospel of Mark. When the unclean spirits recognize Jesus, he orders them to keep silent (1,25.34; 3,12). Jesus likewise tells the leper he cures not to say anything, but his words have the opposite effect (1,43–45; cf. 5,43). Nothing can stop the advance of the Good News; it is like a seed that grows by itself and becomes a magnificent tree (4,26–32).

In the context of this inexorable expansion there are nevertheless different modalities. When people come to him in search of healing, Jesus generally consents to their request and then sends them away: "go home" (2,11; cf. 5,19); "go in peace" (5,34); "see that you say nothing to anyone, but go show yourself to the priest . . ." (1,43; cf. 8,26). In the same way, when the crowds follow him and flock around him (5,24), Jesus heals them (3,10), teaches them (4,2; 6,34) and feeds them (6,30–44; 8,1–10). He does not want them to go away hungry, he has compassion on them (6,34; 8,2), but he does not try to stop them from leaving.

Some encounters, however, have a quite different result. We have already mentioned the call of the first four disciples (1,16–20). The account begins with a verb that evokes once again the pilgrim God: "to pass by, beside." This verb recalls the theophanies before Moses (Ex 33,19.22; 34,6) and Elijah (1 Kings 19,11);

35

in the book of the prophet Amos, it is used to describe the coming of the Lord to save or forgive (Amos 7,8; 8,2; cf. Ex 12,23) and is contrasted with the verb "to pass through the midst" (Amos 5,17; cf. Ex 12,12), used for God's behavior toward his enemies.[4] Passing beside the lake, Jesus sees some fishermen and says to them, "Come follow me!" And at once, leaving their day-to-day existence, they follow him. This short episode emphasizes the fact that Jesus takes the initiative, calling "those he wanted" (3,13),[5] as well as the radical response required from those called.

Those called in this way are thus implicated even more deeply in Jesus' own adventure. They must leave everything to set out in the company of their Teacher. They too become wayfarers, pilgrims on the road. In passing by, Jesus draws them along in his wake. Henceforth, to use the image of Saint Paul, they are part of his victory parade (cf. 2 Cor 2,14).

Among the disciples, Mark accords a special place to the group known as *the Twelve*. The number alludes to the twelve tribes of Israel and thus symbolizes both continuity with the past and something new, recapitulation on a smaller scale and thus a microcosm or seed. Jesus goes up on a hilltop and "calls those he wanted; they came to him" (3,13). The scene transports us to Mount Sinai on the day the covenant was ratified, although in those days only Moses went up to respond to God's call (Ex 19,3.20) while the people remained below.

The role of the Twelve includes two different aspects. First of all they have to "be with him" (3,14a), accompanying Jesus in his travels, watching and listening to him. They are invited to share his life in a way that goes beyond the usual relationship between a rabbi and his disciples. Their progressive formation consists less in the transmission of concepts or theories than in a transformation of their being; it is essentially a school of trust. And Mark strongly emphasizes how incapable the disciples are of fulfilling the mission entrusted to them. In no way can they be considered a human elite. They cannot understand the parables (4,13) or the miraculous signs performed by Jesus (6,52); they are "unintelligent" (7,18), with "hardened hearts" (8,17). Still worse, they are weak in faith: in them, fear often overcomes trust (4,40). And yet they are the true family of Jesus (3,21.31-35; cf. Matt 12,49) because they are "around him," bound to him by a communion stronger than ties of blood or nationality (cf.

6,4). To these individuals, weak like us, God has entrusted the mystery of the Kingdom (4,11).

Rooted in this communion with Jesus, the Twelve are at the same time *apostles* in the literal meaning of the term, that is, people who are sent out. And their task is exactly the same as that of Jesus himself: to proclaim the Good News and to demonstrate its reality by driving out evil spirits (3,14–15). Jesus sends them out two by two throughout the land of Galilee with instructions that underline the urgency of their mission (6,7–11). And then we read that "they went out and proclaimed the message that people should change their ways, and anointed many sick people with oil and cured them" (6,12–13). In this way, too, news of the inbreaking Reign of God expands by leaps and bounds; Jesus' coming leads to the call of other heralds who extend his presence in time and space.

Resistance to the message

If Mark thus places the accent on the dynamism of the new Reality that has come into the world with Jesus and describes its power of expansion, he does not forget that he is dealing above all with an appeal to human freedom. God never forces anyone's heart, and for this reason, almost from the very start, there arises a movement of resistance to the Pilgrim and his message. Is it surprising that the gospels locate this opposition primarily in those who possess spiritual authority and are responsible for interpreting the religious traditions of the people? After all, they are the ones most deeply concerned by these questions. The new beginning offered by God calls into question their customary outlook and opinions and places them before a painful alternative: will they open their hearts to the new and unexpected and so change their lives in consequence, or on the other hand will they close their minds and in the end seek to eliminate the message and the messenger?

Mark shows us this growing opposition in a series of controversies placed at the beginning of his gospel. Already in the second chapter, "some of the scribes sitting there" consider Jesus' announcement of forgiveness a blasphemy, a trespassing on the prerogatives of God (2,6–7). They keep their thoughts to themselves, but Jesus knows what is going on in their minds

37

and responds by healing the man physically, to help them understand by giving them a visible sign. There is a similar reaction when Jesus eats with tax-collectors and other disreputable people, although here "the scribes of the party of the Pharisees" do express their incomprehension, not directly to Jesus, but to his disciples (2,15–17). The two following scenes (2,18–28) witness to the same bewilderment occasioned by the behavior of Jesus' disciples: why do they not observe the laws of fasting, or the Sabbath? These controversies provide Jesus with occasions to reveal his identity more clearly by the use of images. He is the Physician come to heal the sick, the Bridegroom whose simple presence is a source of deep joy (here the wedding banquet, one of the most traditional images of the age to come, is discreetly alluded to; cf. Luke 14,15; Matt 22,2; 25,1ff). He is also the Lord of the Sabbath, who dares to compare himself to King David. These verses contain in addition a reflection on the newness of Jesus' message, which is compared to new wine that can cause old wineskins to burst (2,21–22).

This series of controversies comes to a climax in the story of the healing of a man with a shriveled hand at the synagogue on the Sabbath day (3,1–6). Here the ill will of Jesus' opponents is evident: "they were observing him closely . . . to accuse him." The true significance of the affair is finally revealed. At this point we are witnessing, not an intense but sincere dispute to reach a deeper understanding of the truth, but rather a clear choice between life and death (cf. 3,4). The hearts of Jesus' adversaries have become hardened; since they refuse to see they are now blind, and consequently the healing strikes them like a mortal blow that leaves them only one course of action: "The Pharisees went out and at once plotted together with the Herodians against him, how they might put an end to him" (3,6). Opposition to God's work makes strange bedfellows, such as these two groups with diametrically opposed world-views.

The fact that the party of the Pharisees is often mentioned as one of the principal adversaries of Jesus is a detail whose tragic significance is rarely grasped. Christians, basing their opinion exclusively on a few gospel texts taken out of context, are accustomed to viewing the word "pharisee" as a mere synonym for "hypocrite"; this definition has even found its way into the dictionaries. As a result, we are unable to appreciate the full extent of the drama recounted in the pages of the gospels. In fact, of all the different groups among the Jewish people at the time of Jesus, the Pharisees had good reasons to form a natural clientele of Jesus. Pious men living in expectation of the Kingdom of God, they strove to hasten its coming by putting the Word of God, the Torah, into practice as far as possible in the concrete circumstances of their lives. And it even seems that, reading between the lines, we can detect in the gospels a preliminary period when Jesus and the Pharisees got along well.[6] As an example, we have only to remember the Pharisees who warned Jesus against the threats of Herod (Luke 13,31). Bible scholars, moreover, for the most part agree that, in purely chronological terms, Mark 3,6 comes much too early and must in fact refer to a later period of Jesus' ministry. For at a certain point there was in fact a split; this split grew wider and continued even after the death of Jesus when, after the destruction of the Second Temple in the year 70 of the common era, the tendency represented by the Pharisees began to consolidate and restore Judaism on the basis of its own traditions. This later situation of hostility between those who followed the teachings of Jesus and those who did not has left its mark on the gospels, despite significant exceptions like Nicodemus (John 3,1; 19,39) and Saul of Tarsus (Phil 3,5).

Why did things happen in this way? According to the gospel accounts, including the controversies we have just examined, the Pharisees are especially shocked by Jesus' attitude towards the precepts of the Torah: the laws of purity (cf. Mark 7,1–4), fasting, the Sabbath, and so on. Jesus for his part accuses them of confusing simple human traditions with the Word of God, of interpreting the Law in a superficial way that distorts its true meaning (7,6–13; cf. Matt 23). Jesus himself behaves with sovereign freedom towards the commandments of the Torah, like someone who feels totally at home and not like a passing stranger or a guest. He demonstrates the liberty "not ... to destroy or to overturn, but to go straight to the essential."[7] And so, in refusing to allow an infirm man to suffer on the Sabbath, Jesus reveals himself as truly the "Lord of the Sabbath" (2,28). He reveals the true meaning of that day: it is the Lord's Day, the God of life, the God who wants to give human beings the fullness of life—and this Day is being fulfilled right now, in the *kairos* of the coming of the Kingdom and its herald.

An even deeper source of disagreement between Jesus and

the Pharisees comes to light in the account of the call of Levi and the meal at his home (2,13–17). Jesus' propensity to go toward those who are furthest away from God and most in need of healing is the antithesis of the Pharisees' tendency to mark clearly their distinction from others; their name itself can be translated "the separated ones."[8] Let us be careful not to carica-ture their motivations, which were not fundamentally negative ones. They were not interested in excluding anyone from com-munion with God; on the contrary, the gospel itself tells us that "they cross[ed] sea and land to make a single convert" (Matt 23,15). Their tendency toward separation was simply the other side of their deep desire to study and to live out the Law in all its purity and its fullness. This implied in their eyes, as a neces-sary consequence, remaining apart from all those who did not want—or were not able—to accept the same rigorous standards. This distance was thus an expression of their seriousness, of their horror of compromises. Jesus, however, followed a com-pletely different scale of priorities. What mattered most for him was manifesting the unconditional mercy of God, even more apparent where it is least deserved (and who can deserve it?). Beyond a common concern for the affairs of God, beyond a different way of treating his revealed Word, in the final analysis what separated Jesus and the Pharisees was a different under-standing of who God is. They too were invited to change their hearts and their priorities, to welcome into their lives the utterly free love of God. Tragically, this change of heart is often most difficult for those who possess the most, who have gone furthest along a certain road and have acquired more spiritual baggage.

Beyond the borders

It is of the utmost significance that a basic reason for the divi-sion between Jesus and the Pharisees was his propensity to go toward those who did not follow the ways of God, the com-mandments. In fact, every form of exclusivism whatsoever is utterly foreign to Jesus' way of acting and to the dynamism of the Kingdom whose coming he proclaims. Following its deepest logic, the way of Jesus tends to surpass all human barriers and to transform obstacles into starting-points for a new and wider field of activity.

We have already noticed that among his compatriots, Jesus appears irresistibly drawn to those who are most in need, those who seemingly are furthest from the love of God. Constantly he is found in the company of "unclean" people—lepers, tax collectors, prostitutes—without imagining in the least that he can be "contaminated" by them. The influence moves in the other direction: if Jesus touches a leper, that person's skin is cleansed (1,40–42). And these outcasts know that Jesus accepts them and loves them for themselves (2,15b). The fact that he chooses as one of his intimates Levi, a tax-collector, a member of a particularly despised group for political, religious and moral reasons, is a telling example of this (2,14). And the following scene, where we see Jesus at table in his house with "many tax-collectors and sinners" is still more stupefying when we recall the deep significance in those days of taking a meal together. Sharing food in this way implied recognizing the deep bond that existed between those seated at the same table. In this house, then, Jesus creates and expresses a fellowship based not on the merits of the participants nor on a common belonging in purely human terms but solely on the unconditional mercy of God (cf. Matt 9,13) manifested in his coming (Mark 2,17). If, in Jesus, God comes toward those who are furthest away from him, it follows that his love is a source of healing for all.

The paths of the Kingdom even lead Jesus to travel beyond the borders of the land of Israel. As in the expansion of the Good News in the first chapters of the gospel, this is presented less as an explicit decision on Jesus' part than as a consenting to laws of which he does not seem entirely master. We can sense elements of hesitation in him (7,27.36; 8,9b), as if the time for this wider mission had not yet arrived. His excursions beyond the borders of Israel thus represent a kind of symbolic anticipation of the future.

Jesus' first visit to Gentile territory is a crossing of the lake to "the region of the Gerasenes" (5,1–20). The story shows us the pagan world seen through Jewish lenses. It is indeed an upside-down universe, where men live like wild beasts, where pigs, the most unclean of all animals, graze on hilltops, traditionally holy places. In this looking-glass world, Jesus drives away the impure spirits and restores a semblance of order, but the inhabitants do not want him to remain in their territory. For his part, Jesus refuses to take the man he has healed as one of his disciples,

41

but sends him back home to proclaim the Lord's mercy to his own people. Although Jesus brings healing to this region just as he had done in his own land, this represents only a short interruption of his work in the midst of his own people.

A short while later, Jesus takes another trip outside the frontiers of Galilee (7,24ff). It is apparently not for the purpose of proclaiming the Good News of salvation, but rather in order to be alone with his disciples after a rather lively altercation with the Pharisees: "Entering a house, he did not want anyone to know it ..." (7,24b). But his discretion is useless, for the news of the Kingdom has preceded him and has had its usual impact: " ... but he was unable to remain hidden." A pagan woman comes to him and asks him to heal her daughter. Jesus' reply makes clear the complexity of his attitude concerning the widening of his mission beyond Israel: "Let the children first eat their fill, for it is not right to take the children's food and toss it to the little dogs." This is not a flat refusal, but an acknowledgement of the priority due to his people. It is significant that Jesus uses the expression "little dogs, puppies" to refer to the non-Jews. We should not consider this as an insult, but rather as a recognition that they too belong to the family, though they are not of equal status with the Jews. To call pagans "dogs" was common enough in those days when a universal vision was the exception rather than the rule; by replacing the word with its diminutive, Jesus transforms the insult into an expression of tenderness and possibly even adds a note of humor. Can we detect as well here the echo of an inner debate in Jesus? In any case the woman's response, her trust and her hope, cuts through the difficulty and provokes the announcement of healing.

The two following events, in all probability, likewise take place in pagan territory. Jesus heals a deaf-mute (7,31–37), and later feeds a large crowd with seven loaves of bread (8,1–10) just as he had done earlier for his own people (6,30–44). Here the compassion—the motherly love—of Jesus is the reason for the miracle; he cannot send away hungry people who have come "a long way" (8,3b). The expression *apo makrothen* ("from a long way off") is a discreet allusion to the gathering of all the elect expected on the Day of salvation (cf. Isa 60,4) and prefigured in this meal. In this way we see that the laws of the Kingdom, to which Jesus submits his entire existence, lead to a continuous widening of horizons, even if Jesus himself is fully aware that his own fate will be decided within Israel, and in fact at the very center of the nation, in the holy city of Jerusalem.

Matthew: Jesus, universal Teacher

The other two synoptic gospels each retain the basic perspective of Mark on the Galilean ministry of Jesus while adapting it to their own specific concerns. Matthew, for his part, is less interested in the way of Jesus than in a *synchronic* presentation of him as teacher and healer, fulfillment of the Scriptures and gatherer of a new community. Inspired by motives that are more doctrinal and systematic than historical, Matthew structures his gospel in the form of long discourses separated by narrative material; the discourses come from a source unknown to Mark. As teacher and judge, Jesus in the first gospel is sometimes *seated* (Matt 5,1). People *come up to him*, almost never the opposite, and even *bow down before him* (8,2; 14,33 etc.).[9] This majestic being is nevertheless still the Pilgrim, with no place to lay his head (8,20). He travels throughout Galilee followed by huge crowds (4,23–25). He is also the Servant spoken of by the prophet Isaiah, who fulfills his mission in utter discretion (12,15–21). He is, finally, *ho erchomenos*, the One-who-comes (3,11; 11,3): by the use of this messianic title Matthew sums up in a word the portrait of Jesus given by Mark.

While still retaining the priority of the proclamation of the Good News to Israel (Matthew is the only one of the evangelists to report these words of Jesus to the Twelve (10,5b-6; cf. 15,24): "Do not take the road of the Gentiles, and do not enter a Samaritan city. Go rather to the lost sheep of the house of Israel"), the first gospel clearly indicates its universal significance. Matthew introduces the Galilean ministry of Jesus by a quotation from Isaiah (4,12–16) which explains the geographical import of the Gospel's beginnings: the light shines first of all in "Galilee of the nations" on the very edge of the Promised Land, a territory where Jews and Gentiles live side by side, and thus an image of the entire world. The following summary (4,23–25) describes the progress of the light: Jesus goes throughout *all* of Galilee, teaching and healing the sick; his fame spreads *all* over Syria. People bring to him *all* who are ill, and large crowds from everywhere follow him. Although here Matthew follows for the most part the framework of Mark, he emphasizes even more strongly the universal character of Jesus' mission.

At the same time, Matthew speaks whenever possible of Jesus' *rejection* by members of his people, notably its religious establishment. When he laments their refusal to accept his message, Jesus adopts the language of the prophets of Israel. To take one example, there is his use of the expression "this generation" (11,16; 12,39.41; 17,17; cf. 3,7; Mark 8,12; Ezek 2,5; Deut 32,5; Isa 1,4), which underlines the distance separating the messenger of God and the recalcitrant hearers. "This generation" considers Jesus "a glutton and a drunkard, a friend of tax collectors and sinners" (11,19), but they are "hypocrites" whose religion is only an outward show (6,1 etc.), "wise" and "clever" people insensitive to the mystery of the Kingdom (11,25).

Matthew describes the refusal of Jesus and his message first in general terms. The "cities of Israel" do not welcome the Gospel (ch. 10) and are unable to grasp the import of what they have seen (11,20–24). But it soon becomes clear that Jesus has in mind above all the "scribes and Pharisees," a stereotyped expression used by Matthew to refer to the leaders of the nation. They ask for a sign while at the same time missing what is happening right before their eyes (12,38–42). They "see without seeing" (cf. 13,13–15) and thus can be compared to "the blind leading the blind" (15,14). These men are contrasted with the disciples, the "little ones" to whom God has revealed his secrets (11,25) and who are declared "happy" (5,1–11; 13,16). At the other extreme from the "yoke of the Torah" preached by the Pharisees and their austere, even rigorous teachings, the yoke and the teaching of Jesus are a source of comfort, a balm for all who suffer (11,28–30).

In thus speaking of the universality of Jesus' way and the opposition to his message, Matthew develops seeds already present in the gospel of Mark and almost certainly going back to Jesus himself. But Matthew's particular way of structuring these two themes is motivated above all by pastoral and doctrinal concerns. First of all, the emphasis on the mission to the Gentiles and the break with the synagogue undoubtedly reflects the situation in Syria in the 80s, when most probably this gospel was being composed. Secondly, there is clearly a doctrinal and systematic motivation behind the way Matthew combines the theme of Jesus' rejection by his own people (seen in its extreme form in his death on the cross[10]) and the widening of the Kingdom to all the nations (a consequence of the Resurrection). The retrospective vision of the evangelist thus discerns the seeds of the paschal mystery from the very beginning of the ministry of Jesus.

After the Sermon on the Mount, for example, in the very first miracles he recounts, Matthew places between two Markan episodes the account of the healing of the servant (or child) of a centurion, a pagan soldier (8,5–13). Jesus responds immediately to his request: "I will go and heal him." But the centurion feels unworthy to have him come; a mere command from Jesus would be enough. This provides Jesus with an opportunity to praise the faith of this non-Jew and to state one of Matthew's favorite theses:

> Truly I tell you, in no one in Israel have I found such faith! I say to you that many will come from the east and the west, and will sit at table with Abraham, Isaac and Jacob in the Kingdom of heaven, while those for whom the Kingdom is intended will be cast into the outer darkness, where there will be weeping and gnashing of teeth. (8,10b-12)

God will bring good out of evil: the tragedy of Israel's refusal will permit human beings from the four corners of the earth to enter the Kingdom. In the versions of this story told by Luke and John, this conclusion is absent. In Luke's gospel, the "Jewish elders" even serve as intermediaries between Jesus and the Roman, explaining that he is a friend of their nation and its religion (Luke 7,3–5). For John, the man becomes a royal official, and therefore most probably a Jew; his wish to see "signs and wonders" is criticized by Jesus (John 4,46–54). This episode is a good example of how traditions rooted in the life of Jesus receive different emphases according to the concerns of each gospel writer.

We have seen how Matthew readily highlights the understanding and the good will of certain Gentiles, which put that of Jesus' own compatriots to shame. This is shown in another saying he reports where "this (unbelieving) generation" (here it refers to some Pharisees who ask for a miraculous sign) is compared unfavorably to the people of Nineveh and the Queen of

45

the South. They were able to interpret the signs of the times, "and here there is something greater . . ." (12,38–42). In this way the coming of Jesus, the great Gatherer, in fact leads to a new division, because it obliges people to choose to be with him or against him (cf. 12,30). That is why Jesus uses the image of a sword—an object that separates—to describe his mission (10,34–36; cf. Luke 2,34–35; Heb 4,12).

Luke: the stages of salvation

If Matthew offers us above all a synchronic presentation of Jesus, showing us from the very beginning all the major themes of his message on account of their importance to the Christian community of a later day, Luke, for his part, is more concerned with the progressive evolution of the spread of the Kingdom; his outlook is essentially *diachronic*. His historian's mentality is evident from the start, in the prologues to his works (Luke 1,1–4; Acts 1,1). It would be a mistake, however, to attempt to understand Luke's historiography according to modern criteria for the reconstruction of the past. For he too does not hesitate to systematize, to simplify his data in order to fit a theological framework. But in his case, it is in order better to indicate the successive stages that the mission of Jesus must undergo. In writing his gospel, Luke keeps blocks of Markan material, placing them between sections borrowed from other sources. It is extremely significant in this respect that Luke eliminates systematically everything in Mark that takes place outside of Galilee and Judea. There is one exception to this, for he retains the account of the healing of a possessed man on the other side of the lake, an episode clearly unfavorable to the pagan world. In this way Luke wishes to indicate that the time has not yet come for the widening of the Kingdom to the Gentile world: that will be a consequence of the fulfillment of Jesus' mission on earth. His death and resurrection will prepare this new beginning by the gift of the Spirit at Pentecost, a further stage described in great detail by Luke in the book of Acts.

At the beginning of Jesus' public life in Galilee, Luke places an event that sums up for him the entire course of his mission. This event, the account of his visit to the synagogue in his home town of Nazareth, occurs later in the chronologies of Mark and

Matthew. For Luke, however, it serves as an admirable "logical" starting-point for Jesus' career. His ministry begins really and truly among his own people. Jesus *comes* to his home town, more exactly to its religious center, the synagogue, reads the Scriptures and announces their fulfillment "today" (4,16–22). In this way, Luke emphasizes from the very beginning both the continuity of God's plan and the different stages it must undergo, the preparation and the fulfillment. But immediately things become more complicated: Jesus angers his compatriots by telling them that the salvation he brings is not for them here but for others, farther off. This is an extremely condensed way for Luke to sum up God's designs, including both Israel's refusal and the proclamation to the Gentiles. In the Bible, in fact, the consequences of God's activity are often described as already present in the divine intention that lies behind it (see e.g. Isa 6,9–10). This is hard for us to understand, since no distinction is made between cause and effect, between God's initiative and human freedom, as we are in the habit of doing.

The amazement of the residents of Nazareth turns into anger; they drive Jesus out of the town and bring him to a place from which they intend to hurl him to his death. The violence of his contemporaries and the passivity of Jesus are underlined by these verbs, which prefigure clearly the end of his earthly life in a not too distant future. This is not, however, the way the story ends, but instead by these surprising words: "But he, passing right through their midst, went his way" (4,30). An anticipation of the Resurrection all the more striking because it remains unexplained. For our topic it is significant that the Resurrection is described as a passing through—a "passover"—the midst of a hostile people and then as a journey, in other words as a liberation and as a pilgrimage, a renewal of the Exodus from Egypt and the crossing of the desert. The announcement of a fulfillment, enthusiasm followed by growing hostility, an attempt to put to death and a final liberation: these are the stages of the gospel according to Saint Luke.

Luke pays as much attention as Mark to the explosion of the Good News at the beginning of Jesus' ministry, and he does so in a very concrete fashion. Jesus comes and acts "in the power of the Spirit" (4,14; cf. 4,1.18 etc.). For Luke, the Spirit is a dynamic reality endowed with its own logic, a tangible "power" or "force" by which Jesus heals and touches people's hearts

(5,17; 6,19; 8,46). By his own breath of life, God is thus fully present on earth through the activity of Jesus. By the coming of this "great prophet," the pilgrim God dwells in the midst of his people (7,16; cf. 1,68; John 1,14). Jesus cannot remain in one place, for God sent him to proclaim the Good News of the King-dom elsewhere too (4,42–43).[11] The Lord thus lives as a pilgrim (8,1); he goes from place to place and serves as a gathering-point for "large crowds" that come to listen to him and receive from him a fullness of life (5,15–16; 8,4 etc.).

A final feature that Luke brings out in his portrait of Jesus is his *compassion* and his concern for the *outcasts* of the society of his day. Jesus brings the only son of a widow back to life (7,11–17); he praises the justice of tax-collectors (7,29); he has no harsh words for his family (cf. Luke 8,19–21 and Mark 3,31–35). And Luke pays greater attention to *women*, mentioning their presence from the very beginning in the company of Jesus and the Twelve (8,2–3; cf. Acts 1,14), an unusual practice for the time, and not neglecting their presence in the parables told by Jesus (e.g. 15,8–10; 18,1–5).

Using a diversity of languages and images, the synoptic gos-pels thus describe for us the pilgrim God, the God of Israel, who comes to his people in a simple human life. Jesus is "the One who comes," and his coming is not in order to mete out a harsh judgment or to divide humanity into two camps, but rather to offer a fullness of life. Jesus comes to make present, by his words and by his deeds, an almost inconceivable reality, a God whose deepest mystery is his unconditional love, a God who invites all people to a new beginning in the sharing of his own life.

This reality of which Jesus is the bearer and the incarnation is extremely dynamic. One after another, it tends to break through all the barriers set up by human beings to defend or to justify themselves. It "impels" (cf. Mark 1,12) Jesus to set out con-stantly on the road, to live a pilgrim's life full of unexpected adventures. Like the sower who goes out to sow his seed in all directions, like the physician who hurries toward those who are most gravely ill, Jesus' coming is determined solely by its goal, by the fullness of life it makes possible.

Jesus' life possesses a power of attraction. His coming into the world causes a "coming" of others to him. They come for many different reasons, and often for mixed motives, which run the gamut from simple curiosity to an authentic desire to go beyond oneself in a communion with God. Around him gather crowds of people in search of comfort or healing (Mark 3,20; 4,1; 5,21 etc.), struck by the "natural" authority that emanates from him (Mark 1,22). And among all those who come, some are mysteriously invited to take part in his ministry. They accompany him and in their turn are sent to others to bear witness to the new reality they have discovered.

In all this, there is perhaps nothing very startling. But slowly, another dimension of Jesus' pilgrimage appears and becomes more important. This other dimension runs contrary to the progressive and peaceful expansion of the Kingdom of God. The fountain of water will not automatically, with no problem, become a river that feeds a great lake. On the contrary, as Jesus goes further in his mission, a *resistance* grows as well against himself and his work. Although it is meant for all without exception, the Good News encounters a refusal from some and thus leads to a division. At first, this seems simply to be a matter of understanding: the disciples around their teacher are thus distinguished from "those outside" for whom the message remains an enigma (Mark 4,11). But in the final analysis it has much more to do with a fundamental choice, a refusal to open one's heart to the unimaginable newness of the message and to change one's life in consequence. Fear and incomprehension turn into violence, into the imperious need to get rid of the troublemaker. The slow, inexorable progression of the Kingdom of God takes on more and more the appearance of a bitter struggle between life and death. For the evangelists this is evident from the very beginning, as when they show Jesus casting out evil spirits or comparing himself to someone who enters a strong man's house to tie him up and rob him (Mark 3,27). Little by little, this opposition will determine to an ever greater degree the way of Jesus and the progression of his Gospel.

Questions for Reflection

1. What are the resemblances and the differences between the vocation of Abraham (Gen 12,1–4) and the calling of the first disciples of Jesus

49

(Mark 1,16–20)? What do we learn about the life of faith by comparing these two events?

2. The healing of the sick is an important sign by which Jesus reveals his identity. In Mark 2,1–12, the physical curing of a paralyzed man becomes the sign of a much deeper form of healing known as forgiveness. Where, in our lives, do we need this kind of healing? Where can we find it? How can we, today, as followers of Christ, accomplish gestures of healing and forgiveness in our own situations?

3. Jesus' coming to earth causes others to come to him. What attracts me, personally, in Jesus and his message? How can I deepen a personal relationship with him?

4. Jesus' call widens our horizons; it invites us continually to break down walls and to move toward a universal communion. In reflecting on my own journey, where do I see signs of this widening? Can I specify some of the stages? Are there any resistances or barriers to this openness in me and around me? What is the particular challenge for me at present in order to move toward this universal outlook?

Notes

[1] The parallel is even closer between the Gospel and the Jewish Targum, paraphrases of the Scriptures in Aramaic used at the time of Jesus by Jews who could not read Hebrew. The Targum of Isa 52,7 reproduces the end of the passage in this way: " . . . who says to the community of Zion: 'The Kingdom of your God has become manifest!'" (Strack-Billerbeck III, 8). See Heinz Giesen, "Jésus et l'imminence du Règne de Dieu selon Marc," in *La Pâque du Christ, Mystère du salut. Mélanges F.-X. Durrwell* (Paris: Cerf, 1982), p. 98.

[2] In the Greek world, the expression *euangelion* was used especially for events of major importance such as victory in a war, the birth or the enthronement of an emperor. See art. *"euangelion"* (G. Friedrich) in Gerhard Kittel (ed.), *Theological Dictionary of the New Testament*, Vol. II, pp. 721–725.

[3] The Greek verb *metanoein* is customarily translated "to repent," and its cognate noun *metanoia* "repentance" or "conversion." But in the course of centuries, these English terms have acquired layer upon layer of pious connotations that insulate us from the authentic meaning of the gospel message. *Metanoia* is not a moralistic act, nor is it primarily negative. It involves "a fundamental reorientation of the whole personality" (A. Richardson), a transfiguration of one's basic outlook and one's values, a turning away from a previous way of life

and a turning to God in confident trust as a result of the encounter with the power of divine love. Cf. art. *"metanoeō, metanoia"* (J. Behm, E. Würthwein) in Kittel, Vol. IV, pp. 975–1008, esp. pp. 1000–1003.

[4]See Harry Fleddermann, "And He Wanted to Pass by Them (Mark 6:48c)," *Catholic Bible Quarterly*, Vol. 45, no. 3 (July 1983), p. 389–395.

[5]Jacques Guillet, *Entre Jésus et l'Eglise* (Paris: Seuil, 1985), p. 44–46, 48, emphasizes Mark's use of the verb "to make" to express the brand-new, unexpected aspect of Jesus' activity. "I will make you fishers of human beings . . . And he made Twelve" (Mark 1,17; 3,16). "It is a feature that immediately distinguishes his disciples from those of the rabbis . . . the verb 'make' rather naturally recalls the 'I will make you into a great nation' of Gen 12,2."

[6]This is the thesis of W.D. Davies, "Matthew 5:17,18," in *Christian Origins and Judaism: A Collection of New Testament Studies* (London: Darton, Longman and Todd, 1962), pp. 31–66.

[7]Guillet, p. 92.

[8]As a matter of fact, we do not know with any certainty whether the Pharisees employed their name in this sense. There is a historical problem regarding the identification of this movement which was a forerunner of rabbinical Judaism. For their part, the rabbis called their precursors "the wise men" (*hakamim*). Were the Pharisees (*perushim*) *hakamim* who were extremists, separatists? Was it a name given them by their opponents? See the careful study of John Bowker, *Jesus and the Pharisees* (Cambridge: The University Press, 1973).

[9]Béda Rigaux, *Témoignage de l'évangile de Matthieu* (Paris: Desclée de Brouwer, 1967), p. 253–255.

[10]Not, of course, that the Jewish people, either individually or collectively, was solely or primarily responsible for the death of Jesus; one has only to remember that crucifixion was a Roman form of execution. But for the New Testament writers, Jews themselves for the most part, the theological and psychological problem was not the fact that pagans would reject "the consolation of Israel" (Luke 2,25)—that could occasion no surprise—but that the chosen people itself as a whole did not acclaim Jesus as God's response to their longings. The fact that this theological debate between members of the Jewish people would later serve to justify centuries of anti-Semitism is one of the cruel and tragic ironies of history, and a blot on the collective conscience of the "Christian" West.

[11]This text (Luke 4,43b) is a good example of the "divine passive." For the Jews, the name of God is surrounded with such respect that it was normally spoken only once a year, by the chief priest on the Day of Atonement. In general, different turns of phrase were used to avoid speaking directly of God: euphemisms (Mark 14,61 the Blessed One; Mark 14,62 the Power), circumlocutions (Luke 6,23 "your reward will

be great in heaven") and especially the passive voice. So when Jesus says, "that is why I was sent" he means "that is why God sent me" (cf. also Matt 5,4.6.7; Luke 11,9 etc.).

THREE

Synoptics II, Going up to the City

The first half of the synoptic gospels describes the coming into the world of the stupefying Newness of God. It is basically a centrifugal movement: a going-towards-others that leads others to come in return, although not without resistances. In the second half, the choice for or against Jesus becomes more evident, and the company of pilgrims receives a clearer identity and destination. Jesus is almost always in the company of his disciples, and gradually their pilgrimage becomes a journey to Jerusalem, the religious center of the people of God. It is as if, rather than wishing to run away from difficulties or to start a brand-new religion on other foundations, Jesus is fully aware that his fate is linked with that of his people, come what may.

For the Jewish people after the Exile, Jerusalem and the Temple rebuilt there is the virtual center of the world where, at the end of the age, God will come to rule over his people, or even the whole of humanity. His coming will lead to a judgment, to a titanic battle against the forces of evil for the sake of his chosen ones, a battle perhaps led by his representative on earth, the "Messiah." This problematic of combat and judgment, of death and life is taken up in the gospels, but in a totally unexpected manner. The Son of David enters his City; there is a conflict and a judgment; there is bloodshed that leads to a new life; there is scattering and gathering. But who could ever have guessed beforehand that things would happen just as they in fact did?

A road toward death

In Mark's gospel, the verses 8,27—9,13 form the center and the turning-point, the conclusion of the first part and the introduction to a new stage. For some time now Jesus has been communicating the message of the Kingdom in words and deeds, and some people have left everything to follow him. And yet, the disciples of Jesus find it just as difficult to understand their teacher (8,14–21) as his adversaries do (8,11–13). His behavior is so different from what they expect, since it is rooted in a dimension to which they can have access only by trusting in him. For this reason, comprehension can come to them only as a grace, a gift of clear sight (cf. 8,22–26).

At this moment the miracle occurs that permits a new beginning. Jesus is on the road with his disciples in a faraway region; the geographical situation reinforces the climate of incomprehension and hostility in these days after the death of John the Baptist (6,17–29). All of a sudden he asks them the essential question: Who am I? First on a human level ("what do people say ... ?"), and here a multitude of answers is possible since, by itself, human intelligence seeking God seems doomed to lead to a diversity with no hope of unity. Then the question becomes more personal ("for you ..."), calling for a reply that is not merely sociological but existential and theological. And Peter confesses, in the name of all the others: You are the Messiah, the one Israel has been waiting for for centuries in order to experience its definitive liberation.

Peter's words show that he has been granted the possibility of seeing something far beyond what he is able to understand, humanly speaking. This quickly becomes evident when Jesus begins to explain to the disciples *how* he must live out his mission, by suffering and being put to death. Peter then takes him aside and begins to remonstrate with him, with the result that he hears Jesus speak to him these harsh words: "Get behind me, Satan!" (8,33). Peter has forgotten that the only way for him to understand the mystery of his Teacher is to remain a disciple in an attitude of trust, to "go behind him" instead of attempting to go ahead of him by his own limited views. This is also why, after Peter's confession, Jesus orders them not to tell anyone: he is not implying that they are wrong; he simply knows that this announcement is premature as long as the true meaning of his identity as Messiah has not been revealed. In his version of the event (Matt 16,13–20), Matthew includes words (vv. 17–19) which insist on the importance of Peter's confession for the existence of the Church: from now on a community exists that is founded not on human (and thus fallible) opinions or ideas but on God's own presence and activity in the world.

Even in Mark's account, the reproach made to Peter should not make us lose sight of the fact that an important and irreversible step forward has been accomplished. The recognition of Jesus' identity as God's Anointed makes a new beginning possible. He can now reveal "openly" (8,32) the *meaning* of this identity:

> And he began to teach them that it was necessary for the Son of Man to suffer a great deal, to be rejected by the elders, the chief priests and the scribes, to be put to death and, after three days, to rise. (8,31)

God wants (the expression "it is necessary" (*dei*) is often used in the gospels to refer to the designs of God predicted or promised in Scripture) his Anointed to follow the road of suffering and death, like the Servant of Second Isaiah (PGod 136–145). The Father's will is not motivated by a perverse desire to inflict suffering, for at least since the time of the prophet Ezekiel it is clear that God does not wish anyone to die (cf. Ez 18,23.32; 33,11), least of all his "beloved Son" (Mark 9,7). Rather, it indicates the only way salvation can reach the farthest ends of a world ravaged by hatred and self-centeredness. The pilgrimage of Jesus—and of his disciple (8,34–38)—follows the road of the cross, of the gift of one's life. Only this utterly free gift of self can melt human freedom turned in upon itself and hardened in an attitude of refusal. To put it another way, only love can defeat death.

For there is in fact a victory here, albeit a paradoxical one, and not a failure. In the midst of all the words about suffering and crosses to be borne, Jesus speaks of a resurrection (8,31), of the Son of Man's coming "in the glory of his Father" (8,38) and of "the Kingdom of God come with power" (9,1). Still more, the following episode, that of the Transfiguration (9,2–10), ratifies Peter's confession by revealing fully the identity of Jesus. It is an anticipation, in a climate of theophany (cf. the high mountain v. 2 and the cloud v. 7), of the definitive exaltation of Jesus (cf. the white garments 9,3 and 16,5), prepared by the whole history of Israel, most recently by the coming and the death of John the Baptist, the new Elijah (9,4.11–13). To those closest to Jesus, his secret has now been revealed openly (8,32), but it will take time for it to be grasped and accepted in all its dimensions. Only the resurrection will make this fully possible.

The following section of Mark's gospel (8,31—10,52) is commanded by the way of the cross, obligatory both for Jesus and for his disciple. Jesus spends his time with those who are willing to follow him; the controversies with his opponents are almost entirely absent from these chapters. He teaches his disciples, not always distinguished from the rest of his listeners (8,34; 9,14; 10,1.46; cf. 9,40), his way, the way of the gift of his life (8,34ff). Three times (8,31; 9,31; 10,33–34) he speaks of his death and resurrection, and each time proof of the hearers' incomprehension is followed by a teaching on how they should behave as disciples of his. They are encouraged to carry their cross behind Jesus (8,34), to take the last place and be servants of all (9,35; 10,42–44), thus imitating their Teacher, who "did not come to be served but to serve, and to give his life as a ransom for the multitude" (10,45).

The disciples will drink the same cup as Jesus and be baptized with the same baptism (10,39). The model offered to them, at the opposite extreme from a rich man unable to give up his possessions to journey with Jesus (10,17–25), is that of a little child (10,13–16; cf. 9,36–37). For in the final analysis what matters is trust in Jesus (9,23). A radical choice is called for (9,43ff), similar to that involved in marriage (10,1–12). Those who leave everything to follow Jesus will have a share in a much better life; his entry into the world causes an overturning of human values (10,23–31).

These chapters are filled with images of the *way*. It is as if the literal and geographical allusions to the road (8,27; 9,33; 10,17.32.46.52) and the itinerary (9,30.33; 10,1.32.46) are there to reinforce the conception of the disciple's vocation, his growth in understanding and in the imitation of his master, as a spiritual journey (8,34; 9,38; 10,21.28). For Jesus and his disciples, the entry into life (9,43.45) or into the Kingdom (9,47) is not only a metaphorical journey but a very concrete one, that passes through Galilee (9,30) and Judea (10,1) on its way up to the city of Jerusalem (10,32). There the itinerant preacher will have to confront the leaders of the nation, the establishment, those who hold the political and religious power. As they get closer to the capital, the atmosphere becomes more threatening:

> They were on the road going up to Jerusalem, with Jesus leading the way, and they were apprehensive, and those following were frightened. (10,32a)

The assurance of Jesus, leading the way, is in marked contrast to the fear and uncertainty of the disciples.

The last episode before the entry into Jerusalem, the healing of Bartimaeus (10,46–52), functions as a parable that sums up this section of the gospel. When the blind beggar is called by Jesus, he throws off his cloak and runs up to him. By divesting himself in this way and by trusting in Jesus, he is able to receive new life. After his faith has enabled him to get back his sight, this man who earlier was seated *beside* the road is now *on* the road, following Jesus. In short, what defines the disciple is not his human qualities, his spiritual or material wealth, but solely his readiness to follow the way of the Lord, come what may.

Matthew, in the equivalent chapters of his gospel (16–20), follows the same basic itinerary as Mark. He makes it more relevant to the community he is writing for by adding instructions apt to interest his audience: on mutual assistance and forgiveness among Christians ("brothers," ch. 18) and on celibacy for the Kingdom (19,10–12). Two parables offer an attractive image of the God-who-comes, who takes the initiative in searching for human beings: the lost sheep (18,12–14) and the workers in the vineyard (20,1–16). In this last parable, the landowner goes out four times during the day to hire workers; not until evening does he call them in to give them their wages. Can we not see here an image of the history of salvation, which for Matthew is recapitulated in Jesus? Up to the present, in him, God is going out toward people, but at the end of time he will sit on his throne in the company of his apostles for a judgment (19,28; cf. 25,31–46).

Of all the synoptics, Luke is the one who shows most originality in this part of his gospel. He constructs chapters 9 to 19 as a
long journey up to Jerusalem. These chapters do not follow the
same order as Matthew and Mark, and contain a good deal of
material proper to Luke. If the structure of this section is that of
a "travel narrative"[1], it is clear that here, unlike Mark, the accent
is placed on the destination just as much as on the fact of being
on the road. Already in Luke's account of the Transfiguration
we find this significant phrase: "Moses and Elijah, appearing in
glory, spoke of his departure (*exodos*), which he was going to
bring to fulfillment in Jerusalem" (9,30–31). Jerusalem is thus for
Luke the place of fulfillment, the place of a new Exodus. It is
also the place where he will be "taken up," of his assumption.
This is clear from the formal introduction given by Luke to the
"travel narrative" in 9,51–53. Here is an extremely literal translation of these dense and significant phrases:

> And it came to pass that the days of his assumption were being
> fulfilled, and he hardened his face to journey towards Jerusa-
> lem, and he sent messengers before his face. And journeying
> they entered into a village of Samaritans, to prepare for him.
> And they did not receive him, because his face was journeying
> toward Jerusalem.

The style here is extremely formal and biblical, to mark a new
stage in the mission of Jesus. By means of Scriptural allusions
Luke lends an eschatological coloring to the journey. He describes it implicitly as God's definitive visitation to his people for
the purpose of putting things in order.

In the Greek translation of the Hebrew Scriptures, the verb "to
fulfill" employed in conjunction with a length of time always
refers to the end of the desolation of Jerusalem after the Exile in
Babylon (2 Chron 36,21; Dan 9,2; Jer 25,12; cf. 29,10; Isa 60,20;
Dan 12,13). Similarly, the expression "to harden one's face" in
the Bible can simply refer to the determination to head in a
certain direction (e.g. Gen 31,21; Jer 42,15), but in the prophets
it receives a more specific meaning in reference to Jerusalem.
Jeremiah uses it to predict the destruction of the city because of

its sins (Jer 21,10). Ezekiel, for his part, receives several times from God the order to "harden his face" to prophesy against his people, once against "the mountains of Israel" (Ez 6,2), another time against the false prophets (13,17), and later on against Jerusalem and its sanctuary (21,7). In this, the prophet is in the image of God, who will harden his face against the elders of Israel who have idols in their hearts (14,8) and against the inhabitants of Jerusalem (15,7). Like that of his predecessor Jeremiah, the message of Ezekiel is an announcement of the destruction of the unfaithful nation, and yet it is not without hope, for God will spare a remnant (6,8–10) who will return to him; the ruined City will be restored and given "to the one to whom it rightfully belongs" (21,27(32)). Still later, the Servant of God has to "harden his face" (Isa 50,7) to remain true to his mission despite the hostility of his compatriots. And finally, in a prayer for the restoration of Jerusalem, Daniel asks the Lord "let your face shine on your desolate sanctuary" (Dan 9,17). In short, the "face to face" encounter between the Lord and his people involves both judgment and salvation, destruction and restoration starting from a remnant.[2]

Luke for his part speaks of the face of Jesus, but this face shines with the glory of God (9,29.32). Thus when Jesus journeys (the verb *poreuomai*, "to go, journey," is often found in these chapters, to such an extent that some see it as a technical term in the "travel narrative"[3]) toward Jerusalem, the evangelist has in mind the fulfillment of prophecies concerning God's coming to his city. Like the Lord (God) in Malachi 3,1, the Lord (Jesus) sends messengers before him to prepare his way (9,52). For the post-exilic prophet, this way is the coming of the Lord to his Temple as a purifying fire to judge the wicked and to heal the just (Mal 3,1–5; 4,1–2). The messenger of Malachi, the prophet Elijah come back to life, is identified by Mark and Matthew with John the Baptist (Mark 9,13; Matt 17,12–13; 11,10.14; cf. Luke 1,17.76; John 1,21), but Luke seems rather to see the fulfillment of this prophecy in the sending out of the seventy-two disciples two by two. He is the only evangelist to mention this episode:

After this, the Lord appointed seventy-two others and sent them two by two before his face to every town and place where he was going to go. (10,1)

Their mission is to announce to the cities of Israel[4] the imminent coming of the Kingdom (here set in parallel with the coming of Jesus in 9,52) and to invite them one last time to change their ways. What is at stake for the nation is extremely grave: rejecting Jesus and his disciples is equivalent to turning their backs on God himself at his coming (10,16).

As opposed to Mark and Matthew, who are interested here almost exclusively in the road of the disciple, for Luke the pilgrimage to Jerusalem is thus a final offer of salvation to the people of Israel as a whole, represented by the capital city. The uncompromising words of Jesus are not so much an attempt to make the disciples understand all the dimensions of their vocation as an insistence on the seriousness of the choice set before the nation as a whole. To say yes to Jesus means choosing a pilgrim's life, with no human security (9,57–58); it means allowing all the requirements of traditional piety to take second place (9,59–62; 14,26) in the face of the one thing that matters, listening to Jesus (10,38–42). Israel is now urged to discern "on the way" the signs of the times (12,54–59), to grasp the radicalness of the choice before her (14,28–32; 13,24) and to renounce all she has acquired for the sake of the Kingdom of God (14,33; 18,18–23).

Renouncing, however, does not mean destroying or giving up for good; violence for the sake of the Kingdom (16,16) is always in order to attain a fulfillment (cf. Matt 5,17). The Law still has value (16,17), but its value is that of indicating the road that leads to true life (16,19–31). It is in this context that the enigmatic parable of the shrewd manager must be read (16,1–8). Jesus uses it to teach his compatriots the only correct attitude toward their wealth, spiritual perhaps even more than material: to employ it for the sake of the Kingdom of God. Anything can be a help, but this requires a certain amount of imagination ("shrewdness," 16,8), in other words an inner freedom, the ability to discern the Newness of God beyond the stereotypes and the routines that imprison us. For the midnight hour has struck for Israel: she is losing her position (16,2–3). The banquet is ready (14,17); the door will soon be shut (13,25); the tree cut down (13,6–9). The more powerful man is coming to take possession of the strong man's house in spite of his defenses (11,21–22). And even more clearly, as Jesus puts it to those who have witnessed his acts of healing: "The Kingdom of God has come upon you" (11,20b).

The tragedy of all this—and Luke it well aware of it when he is writing his gospel at a later date—is that this call to conversion will not be heard. The nation as a whole, represented especially (but not exclusively) by its authorities, will not recognize in the main the time of God's visit. "This generation" (11,29.50.51; 17,25) is blind (11,34–35), incapable of seeing the signs of God's coming (11,29–32; 12,56). Its representatives persist in asking for a sign when, in Jesus, the Kingdom is already at hand (17,20–21). Their religiosity is thus shown to be merely an outward form (11,39–44; 12,1); deep down they worship not God but Mammon, their own comfort and well-being (16,13–14; 18,18–25). This is why they are obliged to persecute and kill the prophets sent by God (11,47–51), even though later on they never fail to build them impressive tombs.

To sum up, Luke's account of the journey to Jerusalem depicts Jesus, the worthy successor to the prophets of Israel, as offering one last chance to his people, a chance that from the beginning appears almost futile. This hope beyond all hope characterizes the God of the Bible, who never abandons his own. It likewise explains his suffering, that of a faithful love which only encounters unfaithfulness in return. Jesus takes up this theme in his lamentation over the city of Jerusalem:

Jerusalem, Jerusalem, city that kills the prophets and stones those sent to her, how often did I wish to gather together your children as a mother hen gathers her chicks under her wings, and you were not willing! Look, your house will be deserted. I tell you, you will not see me until the time comes when you say, "Blessed is the One who comes in the name of the Lord." (13,34–35)

Because Jesus' offer is not accepted, his pilgrimage to Jerusalem becomes a journey toward suffering and death. This is not because God wishes this as an end in itself, but because his fidelity leaves him no other solution. To be faithful to his Father and to himself, Jesus "must" go to the center of the nation to confront his people with the reality of God and of their attitude to him. Whatever the consequences of this may be, it is the only possibility for their salvation. Jesus is not interested in starting some brand-new religion, but in living as a true son of the covenant. He explains this to some well-meaning but misguided Pharisees who urge him to run away in order to escape the threats of King Herod:

> At the same time some Pharisees came up to him and said, "Get out and go away from here, for Herod wants to kill you." He replied, "Go tell that fox: see, I am casting out devils and performing cures today and tomorrow, and on the third day I am finished. In any case, today, tomorrow and the following day it is necessary for me to go my way, because it is not possible for a prophet to perish outside of Jerusalem." (13,31–33)

Accepted in a trusting and loving spirit, even death can serve the cause of God and his people.

Salvation for the lowly

In the midst of this somber period, characterized by refusal and incomprehension, there are nevertheless glimmers of a resurrection. Even if, "officially," Israel remains deaf to the entreaties of Jesus, some members of the nation welcome for their part the salvation he offers. Paradoxically, this "remnant" is made up above all of the outcasts of the nation, not its prominent members. Is it an accident that Luke uses the uncommon expression "son/daughter of Abraham" to describe two of these outcasts who find salvation in an encounter with Jesus, the woman possessed by a spirit of infirmity (13,10–17) and Zacchaeus, a chief tax-collector (19,1–10)? Is this not to emphasize the fact that these unfortunate or despised individuals are true descendants of the patriarchs and the prophets, and will sit beside Abraham in "the banquet in the Kingdom" (13,28–29; 16,22)?

For Luke it is this "little flock," heirs of the Kingdom (12,32), that ensures the continuity of the covenant between God and his people. They form the nucleus to which will be added Gentiles "from east and west and north and south" (13,29). Luke is always anxious to show non-Jews as part of the Kingdom. In his version of the parable of the mustard-seed (13,18–19), which is set in this context, Luke does not highlight the contrast between the tiny seed and the huge tree as do Mark and Matthew, but emphasizes rather the birds of the air perching in its branches. And in the parable of the great banquet (14,15–24), Luke mentions two successive invitations after those who were first invited refuse to come: first "the poor, the crippled, the blind and the lame" of the city, then the country-dwellers. For him, the new people will be made up of the lowly of Israel together with Gentiles.

The criteria for belonging to this remnant are not human qualities or merits. On the contrary, as the parable of the Pharisee and the tax-collector shows very clearly (18,9–14), too much confidence in one's own spiritual attainments makes one unfit for the Kingdom of God; only an awareness of one's own limitations and of one's need for God's mercy opens the way. For the pilgrim God always goes toward those who are most in need of him. Luke insists on this key truth of the Bible in chapter 15 of his gospel in three matchless parables: the lost sheep, the lost coin, and especially the prodigal son, which might more properly be called the merciful father. At the center of all of these tales there is the image of an active and generous God who exerts himself tirelessly "to seek and to save what was lost" (cf. 19,10), taking no thought for his dignity or his rights. In the last parable of the three, the father leaves his house twice, once to *run* (!) toward his repentant son, and once to try and convince his elder son, jealous of the "excessive" goodness of his father, to come in and celebrate his brother's return with them. One hopes that the scribes and Pharisees, who "grumbled" (cf. Ex 16,2; PGod 39 and n. 8) on account of Jesus' welcome of "sinners" (15,1–2), were able to get the point of the story.

Since salvation is not achieved by human efforts it is not surprising to see Jesus, when he turns to his disciples, put greater emphasis on the attitude of trust in God than on the demands of the way. "Be without fear," "don't worry" (12,4–12.22–32): that is the main theme of his words. Seek first the Kingdom of God (12,31); pray to the Father without ceasing (11,1–13; 18,1–8) and God will give you all you need (11,8), material things (12,29–31) but above all the Holy Spirit (11,13; 12,12) or the Kingdom (12,32).

Though the attitude of vigilance, of receptivity to God is primary (12,35–40), it is no less true that for Luke this is the very opposite of passivity. Alertness is demonstrated by the servant who does the work his master entrusted to him before leaving home (12,41–48; 19,11–26). Implicit in these passages there is an accent on the length of time that may pass as well as on the master's subsequent return home: the servant can say to himself "my master is taking a long time" (12,45). Faced with a nation unwilling to receive his message, Jesus had spoken with urgency, insisting upon the imminent approach of the Kingdom. For the little flock of the disciples, which already has had a taste of the joy of salvation (10,17), Jesus emphasizes instead the attitude of confident perseverance that will enable them to put up with every possible delay before the unpredictable coming of the Day of the Son of Man (12,46; 17,22–37).

As Jesus and his disciples approach Jerusalem, the reversal of values brought about by God's coming becomes evident. Two "outcasts" of a radically different sort, a blind beggar and a chief tax-collector, look for Jesus. The former is rebuked for his presumption by "those in the lead" (18,39), while Jesus' welcoming of the latter causes everyone to "grumble" (19,7). Nonetheless both receive salvation. And in the parable of the minas, Luke's version adds a (true) story of a king who, during his absence, is rejected by his people (19,14.27). Likewise, during the "royal" entry of Jesus into Jerusalem (19,29–40), Luke mentions that it is not the inhabitants of the city in general but "the multitude of the disciples" that acclaims Jesus and prepares his coming, whereas the Pharisees attempt to silence them. This refusal to understand and to welcome explains Jesus' reaction at the end of his pilgrimage: he weeps over the city that "was unable to recognize the time (*kairos*) of [its] visitation" (19,44), the City-of-peace that could not find peace (19,42). By his grief Jesus anticipates prophetically the destruction of the Holy City. Even if in recounting the details of this Luke is influenced by the Roman siege of Jerusalem which took place in the year 70, the essential is already contained in the tears of Jesus. By abandoning its God who comes (cf. 19,38), Jerusalem in effect signs its own death warrant. Voluntarily or not, the fate of the city and the fate of Jesus are mysteriously linked; king and nation are united in suffering and death (cf. 23,28–31).

Zion, your King comes to judge

The following section of the gospel according to Mark (ch. 11–13), the days spent in Jerusalem, depicts a time of fulfillment

66

that is likewise a new starting-point. The messianic king, the "Son of David" (10,47.48), enters his city; the Lord enters his Temple to cleanse and to take possession of it. But Israel is unable to recognize the full significance of what is happening to her. God's Anointed is something other and something more than an earthly king, a mere descendant of David (12,35–37). The Temple is called to be "a house of prayer for all the nations" (11,17; cf. Isa 56,7). Perspectives which are new and yet deeply rooted in the Jewish tradition, they upset age-old habits and preconceptions. Jesus' coming contradicts the eternal human attempt to create a god in our image and calls for a widening of horizons, a breaking down of bastions.

The structure of these chapters consists essentially of a series of controversies in the Temple between Jesus and the leaders of the people. In this section everything centers implicitly around the notion of *judgment:* "the chief priests, the scribes and the elders" (11,27) think they are able to judge Jesus on the basis of their understanding of the Torah, but in fact they themselves are judged before a higher court. Judged and found wanting, for in spite of their impressive appearance (12,38–40) they are reduced to silence (12,34b). They resemble a fig tree with no fruit, incapable of satisfying anyone's hunger (11,12–14). For a few days the sufferings and death of Jesus are not mentioned, and one has the paradoxical impression that he is in charge and will emerge victorious. After the trial, the Judge pronounces a verdict on the Temple and on "this generation" (ch. 13). The end of a world is near.

If in Jesus the pilgrim God returns to the midst of his people, and indeed of the entire world, then we are witnessing a turning-point of human history. Since the Exile in Babylon centuries ago, Israel has been longing for this return and coming up with ever more ingenious explanations for the successive delays in its occurrence (cf. PGod ch. VII). In the apparently commonplace event of an itinerant preacher who goes up to Jerusalem for the feast of Passover, the eyes of faith discern the fulfillment of this longing, and the gospel writers describe it in such a way as to bring out its deepest significance. First of all by the itinerary: Jesus arrives by way of the Mount of Olives, where according to Zechariah 14 a royal road will miraculously appear for the coming of "the Lord my God . . . and all the holy ones with him" (Zech 14,5b); there, the Lord will wage a definitive battle against all his enemies (Zech 14,1–5; cf. Joel 3). And as announced by the prophet Malachi, the Lord sends messengers before his face (Mark 11,1; Mal 3,1). These oracles place us in a context of eschatological judgment: the friends of God, a tiny remnant undergoing a cruel trial, will receive their liberation, while their enemies will be routed.

At the same time, the manner in which Jesus arrives in the city shows clearly that his kingship and his judgment have a quality all their own, far different from all human power and violence. By choosing to enter Jerusalem riding on a donkey, Jesus evokes one of the last messianic oracles found in the prophets of Israel (Zech 9,9–10): the portrait of a poor ('ani) king, pure transparency before God, who comes to proclaim peace after God has eliminated all the weapons of war from his chosen people; his kingdom of peace will extend to all humanity (cf. PGod 178–179). And "Daughter Zion" (Zech 9,9), personified by the crowd (of disciples? cf. Luke 19,37), exults and shouts for joy for her king, acclaiming him as the One-who-comes and bringer of the Kingdom-that-comes (Mark 11,9–10). Following this, Jesus enters the city and goes straight to the Temple. Mark tells us that he looks around like a proprietor coming to take possession of his home. Surprisingly, however, he does not remain but all at once leaves the city; the end is delayed even though it is already quite late (11,11).

In fact, the Temple remains at the center of these chapters. Jesus goes in and out, as if to show that the visit is not yet definitive, or that by itself the Temple is not big enough to hold the promised salvation. In any case it needs to be cleansed: Jesus performs this necessary purification (cf. Mal 3) by chasing the buyers and sellers out of the Temple courts. He quotes Isaiah (56,7) and Jeremiah (7,11) to justify his action, but in addition it is the last oracle of Second Zechariah that is finally fulfilled:

And on that day there will no longer be any merchants in the house of the Lord of hosts. (Zech 14,21b)

The word translated by "merchant" is literally "Canaanite"; the nation's worship is thus implicitly criticized as idolatrous (cf. PGod 178 and n. 26). While proclaiming its allegiance to the God of Israel, Jerusalem and its rulers have been following a god created in their own image. Jesus thus takes up again the old prophetic tendency which looks upon the sanctuary and its cult with a mistrustful eye.

Once the Temple is purified, Jesus can walk around in it (Mark 11,27) and teach. At this point different groups—chief priests, scribes and elders (11,27), Pharisees and Herodians (12,13), Sadducees (12,18)—arrive to put him to the test. They think they can judge him by verifying his knowledge of God and the source of his authority, but already the layout of the scene indicates that the exact opposite is occurring. Jesus is in the Temple and his opponents come up to him, never the other way round. Implicitly they thus take up the attitude of the supplicant who comes to God in his sanctuary in search of an authoritative message from the mouth of his representative. But since their hearts are not transparent (e.g.12,13), they are confounded and their true motives unmasked: lack of faith (11,31; 12,27), hatred and fear (11,18.32; 12,12), jealousy and greed (12,7), complicity with foreign powers (12,13–17). At this time the nation is like a tree without fruit (11,12–14), a vine that must be entrusted to different tenants (12,9). Of course friends of God can still be found in Israel, especially among the poor (12,41–44). But not exclusively: we encounter a teacher of the Torah able to understand Jesus and to judge his Way more essential than Temple sacrifices (12,32–34). Such individuals are signs of the continuity of God's plan at a time when refusal and rupture seem to predominate.

This is the deepest justification for the placing of chapter 13 at this point in Mark's gospel. Suddenly, the story of Jesus' life and death is interrupted in favor of a long sermon on the end largely employing Jewish apocalyptic categories and images. These categories and images were forged in Israel from the time of the Exile onwards, to express faith in God and his promises when humanly speaking no future seemed possible. They became a language to express both the confident trust born of faith and the extent of the power of evil in the world. The promises will be fulfilled in spite of everything but not without a struggle, necessary for "this generation" to disappear (cf. 13,30).

Jesus employs this somewhat perilous language to encourage his disciples by explaining God's judgment concerning his rejection by the official nation, symbolized by the Temple. His words thus provide us with a key to interpret the events he is currently living through. If we translated his thought into terms more accessible to us today it might sound something like this: those who reject the one who is nevertheless God's response to all their longings are clinging to a world doomed to disappear, a world without hope; but to you who accept me I say, do not be afraid; remain faithful to me in the midst of the convulsions of a civilization built on sand that is on its last legs; do not seek to know when the day of your final salvation will arrive but remain alert at every moment, focussed on the only thing that matters. After the definitive encounter between God's Anointed and his people, and before the tragic final act in the events of the Passion, the synoptics thus offer us an interpretation in Jewish categories of the meaning of what is happening. This meaning is "transhistorical," and thus valid for the entire era that will follow.

In the corresponding part of his gospel, Luke follows the Markan framework closely. He eliminates the story of the fig tree, since he has already laid enough emphasis on the judgment of Jerusalem. And in the eschatological discourse of Jesus, Luke, always concerned to indicate clearly the stages of salvation history, distinguishes between the destruction of the city of Jerusalem on the one hand and the signs of the coming of the Son of Man on the other. The former event is a prelude to the "times of the Gentiles" (Luke 21,24) and occurs within an ongoing history. The day of the Son of Man, a day of deliverance for the disciples, is of another order entirely: all that can be done is to "watch and pray" (21,36) so as not to become drugged by the pleasures and cares of the world (21,34), so as to be ready to welcome the approaching redemption (21,28).

For his part, Matthew makes the discourse more eschatological. The disciples ask, not when "all that" will happen and be over (Mark 13,4) but "the signs of your coming (*parousia*) and the end of the age" (Matt 24,3). Once again, where Luke separates the successive stages, Matthew gives a synchronic presentation that brings out the permanent significance for believers of the events. In the same way, immediately before the discourse he includes a long denunciation of "the scribes and Pharisees, hypocrites" (ch. 23). Now in Mark's gospel, the Pharisees were the principal opponents of Jesus during the first part of his ministry, in Galilee; in the capital, they seem to have been less influential. The rulers of the nation belonged for the most part to the party of the Sadducees. Luke thus eliminates any mention

70

of the Pharisees during Jesus' stay in Jerusalem, while Matthew multiplies the references. Perhaps in this way he is alluding to the adversaries of the Christian communities at the time he is writing his gospel some forty years later. We know that after the destruction of Jerusalem and the Temple, the movement of the Pharisees became virtually identical with official Judaism. For Matthew, in any case, the "Pharisees" have become a symbol. They represent the Jewish opponents of Jesus and of his followers much more than any clear-cut historical group of people.

Matthew integrates other stories into these chapters, notably parables, that show the refusal of salvation by the rulers of Israel and its acceptance by the poor and the outcasts: "Truly I tell you, tax-collectors and prostitutes are going before you into the Kingdom of God" (21,31b). The first gospel shows Jesus in the Temple acclaimed by children (cf. Ps 8,2) and healing "the blind and the lame" (21,14–15). These unfortunates come up to him, although traditionally they were not admitted into the holy place (Lev 21,18; 2 Sam 5,8); it is thus clear that a new age is dawning (cf. Mal 4,2). Salvation is a free gift of God, and yet Matthew reminds us that discipleship has its requirements: those who would follow have to be dressed for the wedding (22,11–13), take enough oil for their lamps (25,1–13), and invest wisely the talents bestowed on them (25,14–30), if they are not to exclude themselves from the banquet in the Kingdom (cf. 8,11).

Matthew concludes this part of his gospel with the great scene of the final judgment (25,31–46). Here the evangelist borrows the language of the prophets to explain the ultimate meaning of the gospel, in a manner analogous to what the preceding discourse (ch. 24) had done using apocalyptic images. For Matthew, Jesus is already the cause of a fundamental separation between people based upon their attitude to him (cf. 10,32–34; 11,23–24). Here this truth is projected into an absolute future time, when the Son of Man comes "in his glory" to sit on his throne and judge. This final judgment, however, only ratifies a judgment that has already taken place in the course of history.

Two things should be noted concerning Matthew's account of the judgment. First of all, here there is no longer any mention of the relationship between the chosen people and the other nations, still less of any priority accorded to the former. All peoples, with no mention of Israel, are gathered together and judged. In the prophetic tradition, we find traces of a final battle of the nations against Israel, who emerges victorious (Ez 38–39; Zech 14). We also find a separation within the people of God between the "righteous" and the "wicked." But here the role of Israel seems to have been eliminated, or rather absorbed into the figure of the "Son of Man and all his angels with him" (25,31; cf. Deut 33,2–3; Zech 14,5). Here, the "holy remnant" of the nation is placed with the judge rather than with the judged (cf. Matt 19,28).

Secondly, the definitive criterion upon which the judgment is based lies in the attitude shown towards "one of the least of these brothers of mine." The hungry, the thirsty, the needy and the exploited occupy the place which belonged to Jesus during his earthly life and which the Son of Man himself will assume at the end of time. Jesus recognizes himself in the poorest of the poor, and he recognizes as his own those who minister to them. These two categories come together in the biblical figure of the Servant of the Lord elaborated by Second Isaiah (cf. Matt 12,15–21), a being who in the end becomes one of the lowest of the low, but who does so in order to heal the wounds of all (Isa 52–53). In the final analysis, then, for Matthew, all human history is overshadowed by the figure of the Servant of the Lord. The Son of Man represents the "glorious" revelation by God of what the Servant was in a hidden way (cf. PGod 181). The earthly life of Jesus is already a partial revelation, to those who believe, of what "one day" will be recognized by all.[5]

Evil disarmed

We have seen how the synoptic gospels describe Jesus' journey to Jerusalem for the feast of Passover in terms of a king who takes possession of his city, or even as the definitive and victorious arrival of God to bring about the reign of justice, to inaugurate a new order. They know, of course, that Jesus provides a response to the aspirations of his people recapitulated in Scripture by transforming them at the same time; in him all the fragments bequeathed by the tradition are fused into a new unity, beyond all prior expectations.[6] The end can never be predicted from the lines that lead up to it. Moreover, the inspired authors know that their vision is illuminated by faith. They write retrospectively, in the light of the Resurrection and of Pentecost, and outside of that light things appear quite differently. As a result we are not only confronted with a lack of correspondence between the facts of Jesus' life and the prophetic descriptions of the future found in Scripture. More deeply still, there is a gap between that life and its true significance. This gap remains because Jesus' coming as herald of the Reign of God does not replace faith but instead makes it more necessary than ever. If the life and death of Jesus provides us with an "utterance of things that were hidden" (Matt 13,35), that is not in order to make an act of trust and a radical choice superfluous. On the contrary, when God's secrets are revealed, this trust and this choice are seen to be more essential than ever in order for the revelation to be fully understood. To put it another way, the gospel message is by its very nature a creator of communion; no true understanding is possible from the outside.

It is important to remember all this before considering the final stage of Jesus' pilgrimage during his earthly life—the road to Golgotha, towards the acceptance of a painful death. Here, the disparity between the facts and their significance in the light of faith becomes practically total. The man who was implicitly described as a triumphant king leading his victory parade is in fact, seen from the outside, a criminal led out to be tortured by his executioners, to undergo, like a slave, a shameful death.

That is why, in the account of the passion of Jesus, *irony* occupies such an important place. By its very nature, irony exploits the contrast between the true meaning of an event and its outward appearance. It plays upon incongruity, upon the different outlooks and horizons of the actors in a situation. At the end of Jesus' life on earth, that irony is the only way to take all the different levels into account. It makes it possible to hold together the claims of Jesus, the facts of his life seen from the outside, the reaction of his enemies to the discrepancy between the two, and finally, the true situation in the light of the resurrection. The irony thus exists on several levels, and at times it is almost unbearable.

But before everything is resolved in this final irony, like a complex musical chord where even the apparent dissonances are held together in creative tension, there is a final period of preparation. From the start everything is placed under the sign of the approaching Passover. The most important celebration of the year, Passover recalls the liberation from slavery in Egypt by the "passing over" of the Angel of the Lord and the beginnings of the exodus towards the Promised Land; now it will also be the hour of Jesus' "passion" and his final "passing over" to the one he calls his Father.

Mark and Matthew begin this final period with the account of a woman who anoints Jesus with perfume (Mark 14,3–9; Matt 26,6–13). Luke had used a similar story as a lesson on forgiveness and love (Luke 7,36–50), but here it is presented as a prophetic act: "She has anointed my body for burial ahead of time" (Mark 14,8b). This act is framed by the discussions of the authorities on how to kill Jesus (14,1–2) and by the decision of Judas, "one of the Twelve," to betray his teacher (14,10–11). These contrasting attitudes cause the woman's gesture to stand out even more strongly and give it its full "ironic" significance.

A second step concerns the preparations for the Passover meal. Here again, Jesus appears clearly as the one who is fully in charge, who takes the initiative. He sends his disciples to take possession of "a large upper room, furnished and ready" (14,15) that Jesus calls "my guest room" (14,14). Even if Jerusalem as a whole is not faithful to its God, there does exist at the heart of the capital city a place that welcomes the Messiah, a place where true worship can be offered to God. It is not surprising, then, that, for Luke, the upper room is the starting-point for the Christian community after the ascension of Jesus (Acts 1,13). In that room, Jesus will celebrate a final meal with his disciples, a liturgical means to explain to them the meaning of what is going to happen and to enable them to relive it afterwards.[7]

Like the anointing with perfume, this other symbolic act of Jesus contrasts strongly with its context. It is surrounded by betrayals. Judas plans to hand over his teacher for money; Peter is going to deny him, and all the other disciples will abandon him. Here we are confronted with the final consequences of the reality of evil, the destruction of trust and of love, in a word, scattering (cf. Mark 14,27). Still, everyone's behavior is not on the same level: Peter and the other disciples abandon their teacher out of fear, whereas Judas uses him for his own purposes. This ability to profit from the vulnerability of love makes Judas almost into a personification of evil (cf. Luke 22,3). And yet, in the face of this evocation of absolute evil, and without minimizing its horror (Mark 14,21), the gesture of Jesus offers the only way out:

74

And while they were at supper he took bread, said the blessing, broke it and *gave* it to them saying, "Take it; this is my body." And taking a cup, he gave thanks and *gave* it to them, and they all drank from it. And he said to them, "This is my blood of the covenant, which is shed for the multitude." (14,22–24)

By this totally free decision to give himself, Jesus does the only thing capable of transforming the reign of darkness into the victory of love. He takes the initiative out of the hands of Judas and the chief priests not by a refusal, by running away or by fighting them, but by saying yes to his Father and his loving will. By consenting to die for love, the meaning of that death is radically changed: the "passion" is no longer passive; it becomes the triumphant activity of love, a wellspring of life. Without the last supper, we would not understand the true meaning of Jesus' agony. We would not know that it is a road of life, a paradoxical victory over death from within.

In order for this yes of Jesus to be indeed a victory, it must be not an acquiescence to the views of his enemies but an assent to something of a totally different order. In other words, Jesus can never agree to a murder, even (or especially) to his own, but only to the loving designs of his Father. Before saying his yes, he has to discern in the events that lie before him the way of God for himself and for the world. He has to recognize in them not a blind or malevolent destiny but the face of the Father. We have already seen traces of this in the gospel, without always being able to tell if they go back to Jesus himself or if they express a conviction of the evangelist enlightened by the events of Easter. This is the case, for example, in the predictions of the passion, of the "must" (*dei*), an expression of the Father's will (e.g. Mark 8,31 par; Luke 13,33), and of sayings like Mark 10,45: "The Son of Man did not come to be served but to serve, and to give his life as a ransom for the multitude."

The yes said to the Father and not to evil likewise is evident in the words spoken over the bread and the cup: "This is my body (given) for you" (Paul, Luke) . . . "This is my blood of the covenant, shed for the multitude" (Mark, Matthew). In the face of this network of biblical allusions, too dense for all the different elements to be separated out or to distinguish between what is explicit and what is not, one thing can be said for sure: no one can decide for themselves to be the paschal victim (Ex 12), the sacrifice of the (new) covenant (Ex 24; Jer 31), or the Servant of God (Isa 53)—that can only be a response to a call from God.

The gospels provide us with a final indication of the fact that Jesus' apparent obedience to the destructive will of wicked men is in fact confident trust in the Father in the different meanings of the word "to hand over" (*paradidōmi*), so common in these chapters.[8] Most of the time it is used to refer to the act of Judas, the betrayal of his master out of greed (Mark 14,10.11.18.21.42.44). The word is also employed to describe the stages of the trial of Jesus, handed over to Pilate by the chief priests (15,1.10) and handed over by Pilate to be crucified (15,15). These are everyday uses of the word. But in 14,41, we have in all probability another meaning of the word, easy to miss because of the context in which Judas is so prominent: "The hour has come; see, the Son of Man is being handed over into the hands of sinners." This verse sends us back to the predictions of the passion (9,31a; 10,33), and there the expression is a "divine passive" referring to the activity of God (cf. also Rom 8,32; 4,25). This is a specifically religious use of the verb: in the Hebrew Scriptures, when God hands over an evildoer into the hands of his enemies, it is so that he may experience the consequences of his sin (e.g. Judg 2,14; Ezek 11,9; cf. Rom 1,24.26.28). In Isa 53,6 in the Greek translation, however, a further step is taken: the Servant of God is handed over not on account of his own sins but to take upon himself the consequences of the sins of others. Thus in the Markan use of the verb "to hand over" we can perceive, behind human malice, the saving will of the Father, and consequently the possibility of turning suffering and death into a road to life for all.[9]

This trusting and loving yes, the deepest significance of Jesus' pilgrimage to the cross, was thus prepared and meditated upon a long time in advance. Jesus lives it out in an explicit fashion just before his arrest, in the place called Gethsemani (Mark 14,32–42). There, the most innocent of all men experiences all the power of evil, especially the loneliness it causes, and this imprints a deathly sadness on his soul. We witness his inner struggle in his dialogue with God: the understandable desire to escape the hour of trial, not to have to drink the bitter cup [10]; and, on a deeper level, trust in his "Abba," his loving Father, and thus the free acceptance of his will. Here we are at the opposite extreme from any kind of fatalism, from a grudging assent to the lesser of two evils. What in fact occurs is precisely the opposite: Jesus' trust gives him the confidence that his Father wants what is best for him and for all, even if God's tender care for him is temporarily veiled by the forces of evil. By his act of trust, Jesus is able to recognize even in this hour of darkness the infinitely kind face of the Father, and therefore for him this hour that has come (14,41), the hour in which he is handed over, can also be the hour of the Kingdom, the hour of the Son of Man.[11] By his yes the opening has been made, the path of light traced out; all that remains now is to walk along it.

The passivity of God

The following episodes, on the arrest, condemnation and execution of Jesus, depict the course of this paradoxical pilgrimage, where death and life confront one another and become entangled. Humanly speaking, it is almost entirely a tale of the death of "the Son of Man [who] goes away" (Mark 14,21; Matt 26,24).[12] This is even shown by the syntax of these chapters. Previously, in most of the sentences, Jesus was the subject of active, often dynamic verbs (he came, he arrived, he declared . . .) now we see only passive constructions applied to him: they took hold of him, led him away, brought him in, asked him, led him, spit on him, blindfolded him, struck him, slapped him, bound him, handed him over, (Pilate) sent him (to Herod), (Herod) sent him back, they ridiculed and mocked him, put a purple robe and a crown of thorns on him, led him out, divided up his clothes, sneered at him, insulted him, crucified him. Jesus has become passive, a mere object or plaything that "they" (a use of the plural symptomatic of an absence of moral courage hiding behind anonymity, a perfect example of "mob psychology") can treat with impunity. The appearance of passivity is strengthened by the *silence* of Jesus (Mark 14,61; 15,5), broken only by a few mysterious and even ambiguous words. The official trial comes too late. It is no longer the time for explanations but only for the Servant of God, for the persecuted just man who silently (Isa 53,7; Ps 39,9) puts up with mockery, sure that in the end he will be vindicated by his God (cf. Mark 14,62 par).

It is interesting to note that the principal accusation made against Jesus during his trial concerns his attitude towards the

Temple. In the religion of the Bible, a criticism of the Temple and the eternal human tendency to want to enclose God in the limits of our understanding was a constant theme of prophetic preaching (cf. Jer 7; Isa 66,1–4). But here a further step is taken, since Jesus is attacked above all for having promised a rebuilt sanctuary, a new meeting-place between God and humanity (Mark 14,58).

While Jesus lets himself be led in this way, his opponents are more active than ever. Everyone is united against him, even Pilate and Herod; Jesus brings together these two great enemies (Luke 23,12). And yet the authorities are not able to bring things to a successful conclusion. They cannot find reliable witnesses to testify against him (Mark 14,55–59), and Pilate is about to release him for lack of evidence (Luke 23,13–16). Here, too, irony plays its role: Jesus' enemies do not benefit from a outlook inclusive enough to give them the last word, since such a viewpoint can only be that of God. So, for example, they ridicule Jesus and his claims to kingship, crowning him with thorns (Mark 15,16–20), but this crowning has a significance that goes far beyond their conscious intentions, for Jesus is in fact the humble king who identifies himself with the lowly (cf. Zech 9,9–10). On the one hand, then, Jesus' adversaries make themselves ridiculous and are proven guilty of blasphemy, and on the other, their activity contributes to the fulfillment of God's plan of which they themselves are largely unaware. The notice in three languages that Pilate nails to the cross to irritate the Jewish authorities but that in fact proclaims the universal kingship of Jesus in another example of the same sort (John 19,19–22). As the proverb says, who laughs last, laughs best.

During the passion of Jesus that ultimate horizon, the divine viewpoint that reveals the full meaning of what is happening, is not yet accessible. No one is capable of grasping the irony, or of reading the Scriptures "correctly" to cast all the necessary light upon the subject. Jesus is purely a victim, absolutely alone and helpless in the face of the immensity of evil in the universe. His disciples were scattered by the shock of the arrest (Mark 14,50). Peter follows him from afar, but does not even have the courage to admit his relationship to him. The last words of Jesus (in Mark and Matthew) are an apparent cry of abandonment (Mark 15,34; Matt 27,46), and even though they come from a psalm of trust, nothing authorizes us to conclude that that trust

78

is justified. For Elijah does not come to inaugurate the Reign of God in glory, the Messiah does not come down from his cross, and Jesus dies with a loud cry (Mark 15,35–37). Can we really believe that God would have let his Anointed, his beloved Son, die in such an ignominious manner?

If we are not to falsify completely the Christian message, any contemplation of the way of the cross must give due weight to this dimension of apparent failure. By denying or minimizing it, we turn the Gospel into a utopia, a human optimism; we downplay the seriousness of evil, its irreducible quality, and thus lose touch with reality. It is true that faith gives us the certainty that death is not the last word, and this explains our tendency to leap at once to the other bank of the resurrection in order to cushion the impact of evil on us.

A cut-rate consolation, however, will not do the trick. How many men and women have been turned away from the faith by words of consolation offered with the best of intentions but which sounded to them like an explanation of the inexplicable, the last thing they needed in their hour of darkness? For evil, as those who experience it know well, cannot be explained away; it can never be reduced to a kind of Hegelian antithesis brought in for the sole purpose of reaching a final synthesis. The God of the Bible never explains evil, still less does he attempt to justify or excuse it. He does something quite different, he forgives it, in other words he takes upon himself its consequences to the utmost and responds with love.

This behavior of God revealed in the cross of Jesus permits us to speak of a "transformation" of evil into good, or even of a "happy fault."[13] At the same time, it is essential to understand that such expressions are approximations, or rather short-cuts to describe the consequences of the entire pilgrimage of Jesus from death to life. They include a passing through death, and strictly speaking are only true "on the other side" of death, in God. Applied without discernment to a human situation "on this side," they can serve as a myth, or even a falsehood, that keeps us from discovering and following the true way of Jesus. In any event, they can never lead to the conclusion that evil is justified or is acceptable in God's eyes.

The gospel account of the passion proceeds in a quite different way. The horror of Jesus' torture and death are not watered down, nor are the motives and attitudes of the other participants

79

in the tragedy. The account is sober, exact, "objective." But in the midst of this horror and with infinite delicacy, the inspired author allows a few rays of light to pierce through for those whose eyes have been made sensitive enough by God to perceive them. He does this first of all by means of Scriptural allusions, a classic procedure to indicate that something is in conformity with God's plan. If Jesus is in fact the persecuted Righteous One of the Psalms and the Book of Wisdom (ch. 2–3), the Servant of Second Isaiah (52,13—53,12), the Pierced One of Second Zechariah (12,10 - 13,1), then we are in the presence of something far different than a human failure. In addition, the gospel writer emphasizes details that have little importance in themselves but take on much greater significance in the light of what is to follow. This is something similar to the experience we have on reading a good mystery story for the second time. For example, there are the events mentioned at the moment of Jesus' death: the curtain hanging before the Sanctuary is torn in two, symbolizing the end of the old order and the accessibility of salvation for all; the words of the Roman centurion become a confession of Jesus' true identity; the presence of the women expresses a continuity which holds promise for the future—the scattering has not been complete. The resurrection does not destroy death and its power "on this side," but it places it in a more encompassing context, an ultimate horizon that transforms its meaning. The clearest symbolic expression of this is given by the wounds still visible on the glorified Christ. They are not only visible, they are the means to demonstrate his identity (Luke 24,39; John 20,27). This is something quite different from a kind of magic that would eliminate the necessity of passing through a narrow gate. The gate is still there, but henceforth we encounter it with a different understanding, and with the support of a presence.

The story of Jesus' passion and death ends with his burial. At the center is the tomb, watched over by the women. On the one hand Jesus' passivity is now complete; he is only a "body," or rather a "corpse" (Mark 15,45), entirely at the mercy of others, lying motionless in the tomb, that place of "memory" turned toward the past. On the other hand the scene transmits a strong impression of calm and serenity—the tomb as a place of repose, of quiet and peace after the agony of the day. It is evening, the beginning of the Sabbath, the day when everything finds rest and restoration in God. The contemplative attitude of the women reinforces these two dimensions: they do nothing apparently useful (what can they do now?) but their availability and openness will permit the birth of a new world.

At the end of his gospel, Mark maintains the ambiguity that has been attached to the way of Jesus since the beginning of his journey towards Jerusalem. The discovery of the empty tomb by the women and the announcement of the resurrection awaken in them only fear and the desire to flee (16,1–8). Are we witnessing a road toward death or toward life? For the outside observer, no definite answer can be given with total certainty. This is because the gospel is not a closed, mythical universe, where all the contradictions are neatly resolved at the end. We are dealing instead with salvation history, and this history is still incomplete. It continues down through the centuries, touching the heart of every man and woman who hears the message. Confessing belief in the Risen Christ means believing as well that his road crosses our own and asks for a decision. The written gospel is only a "beginning" (Mark 1,1); it remains necessarily—and intentionally—incomplete (cf. John 20,30–31; 21,25).

Questions for Reflection

1. As soon as Jesus is recognized by his disciples as the Messiah, he reveals to them that he must follow the road of suffering and a violent death, the way of the cross (Mark 8,27–31). Why are these two things so closely connected? Then he continues: "If anyone wants to come after me, let them deny themselves, take up their cross and follow me. For whoever wants to save their life will lose it, and whoever loses their life, for my sake and the gospel's, will save it" (Mark 8,34–35). What do these words mean? How can we put them into practice in our daily lives?

2. In Luke's gospel, the long journey to Jerusalem (ch. 9–19) is presented as a final offer of salvation by God to his people. This offer is not accepted by the nation as a whole, but by a "remnant" made up of the lowly and the outcast. By what "prophetic" signs is God offering salvation to our world today?

3. What is the theological significance, according to the gospel writers, of Jesus' coming to the holy city of Jerusalem and to the Temple? How do they help us grasp this significance?

4. In Mark 13 Jesus explains, in a language that is almost incomprehensible for us, the true, ultimate meaning of his coming to the world. The encounter between God's Anointed and his people leads to divisions, the end of an old order of things and even persecution. How did these things happen during Jesus' life on earth? Why? Are they part of an ongoing process that continues down to our day? What should be our attitude in the face of this situation? What does the advice to "keep alert" mean for us (Mark 13,33–37)?

5. By instituting the Eucharist during the last supper, Jesus reveals the deepest meaning of his life and his death. What is the importance of the fact that, in Mark's and Matthew's gospels, the meal is framed by the announcement of Judas' betrayal and the prediction of Peter's denial (Mark 14,17–31; Matt 26,20–35)? Of the fact that, in Luke's gospel, it comes before a discussion on the meaning of greatness (Luke 22,14–27)?

6. The passion and death of Jesus, the apparent victory of the forces of evil, is in the eyes of faith the victory of love. How do the gospel writers confirm this statement by the manner in which they recount the events?

Notes

[1]See Helmuth L. Egelkraut, *Jesus' Mission to Jerusalem: A redaction critical study of the Travel Narrative in the Gospel of Luke, Lk 9:51—19:48* (Peter Lang Frankfurt/M; Herbert Lang Berne, 1976); Wm. C. Robinson, Jr., *The Way of the Lord: A Study of History & Eschatology in the Gospel of Luke,* A doctoral dissertation submitted to the Theological Faculty of the University of Basle, 1960.
[2]Cf. Egelkraut, pp. 76–80.
[3]Egelkraut, pp. 11–12; Gerhard Schneider, *Das Evangelium nach Lukas Kapitel 1–10* (Güterslohen Taschenbucher Siebenstern, 1977), p. 227.
[4]Because of the mention of Samaria in 9,52 and the number 72 which can stand for the totality of pagan nations, some have seen here a prefiguration of the post-paschal mission to the Gentiles. See Augustin George, "La construction du troisième évangile," *Etudes sur l'oeuvre de Luc* (Paris: Gabalda, 1978), pp. 24–25. It seems, however, that Luke has in mind above all the towns of Israel; Jesus wants to offer them a last chance for conversion before the definitive entry of the King into his City. For Luke the stages of salvation are essential, the "times of the Gentiles" (21, 24) can only come after the offer of salvation to Israel and its rejection (cf. Acts 13,46).

[5]Cf. Xabier Pikaza, "La estructura de Mt y su influencia en 25,31–46," *Salmanticensis*, Vol. XXI, Fasc. 1 (Enero-Abril 1983), pp. 11–40.

[6]Cf. Hans Urs von Balthasar, *Pâques le mystère* (Paris: Cerf, 1981), p. 219: "What is decisive . . . [is] that the *graphai*, the Old Testament as a whole, was found to issue in a transcendent synthesis that could not be constructed starting from it." See also p. 191.

[7]For the link between the Eucharist and our topic, see François-Xavier Durrwell, *L'Eucharistie sacrement pascal* (Paris: Cerf, 1980); François Bourdeau, *L'Eucharistie Pâque du pèlerin* (Paris: Cerf, 1981).

[8]The definitive study on this question is Wiard Popkes, *Christus Traditus: Eine Untersuchung zum Begriff der Dahingabe im NT* (Zürich/Stuttgart: Zwingli Verlag, 1967).

[9]There exists a biblical parallel that helps us understand how the act of "handing over" someone who is deeply cared for can be a sign of faith (faithfulness, trust) and love: the story of the sacrifice of Isaac in Gen 22. Although the word "to hand over" is not found there, in this act of Abraham who did not refuse to give his only son back to God (Gen 22,12.16), the NT writers saw a clear analogy (Heb 11,17–19: "a figure" [*parabolé*] with the act of God giving the most precious thing he could give, his only Son (Rom 8,32; John 3,16; 1 John 4,9). In the primitive confessions of faith we find another formula, "Christ handed himself over" (e.g. Gal 2,20; Eph 5,2; cf. John 10,15–18). This could represent a later stage of theological reflection. Cf. Popkes, pp. 240–257.

[10]Concerning this whole question, which is summed up in the mysterious and ambivalent symbol of the *cup*, see the profound reflections of Jean-Miguel Garrigues, *Dieu sans idée du mal*, (Limoges: Editions Criterion, 1982), especially pp. 123–153.

[11]Is it a mere coincidence that Mark uses exactly the same verb, "to approach" in the perfect tense, to describe the proclamation of the Kingdom in 1,15 ("the Reign of God is at hand") and the arrival of Judas to hand him over in 14,42 ("my betrayer is at hand")?

[12]In the eyes of the two evangelists, this departure is not a mere disappearance, for shortly afterwards they recall the words of Jesus, "After my resurrection I will go before you to Galilee" (Mark 14,28; Matt 26,32). The "going away" (*hyp-agein*) is thus also a "going ahead" (*pro-agein*). Luke, for his part, replaces the word "*hypagein*" by "*poreuomai*" ("to go on one's way, journey"), thus emphasizing the unity between the two aspects of the pilgrimage (Luke 22,22; cf. 4,30). This is one of the "small Johannine touches" we find in the gospel of Luke.

[13]Cf. Garrigues, pp. 79ff.

FOUR

John, Entry into the World, Road to the Father

When we bid farewell to the synoptic gospels and turn to Saint John, we leave behind the step-by-step crossing of the plain for the empyrean heights, for the eagle's eye view. The other gospels are constructed essentially out of short episodes and words of Jesus, strung like beads on a necklace by each evangelist to form a coherent whole. John's gospel resembles more closely a "seamless garment" (cf. John 19,23), a musical composition with themes that emerge and disappear in order to reappear later on, transformed. Past generations of scholars sometimes attempted to explain the particular character of the fourth gospel by the distinction between "spiritual" and "historical" or between Greek and Semitic categories of thought. Today we recognize that these polarities do not at all give us the key to the originality of this work. John does not neglect history in favor of a putative spiritual content; in many cases he offers historical data of very high quality unknown to the other gospels, suggesting the contribution of an eyewitness at least in the early stages of composition. Similarly, the great Johannine themes are all rooted in biblical and Jewish soil. The use of a Hellenistic vocabulary seems to be more a question of style than of anything else, due to the influence of the dominant culture at the time in that part of the world.

John's originality has another basis: it consists in the *contemplative* character of this gospel, his ability to turn the events over and over in his heart in order to penetrate to their deepest significance. The historicity of the facts remains safe, but they are so well assimilated that it is virtually impossible to draw the line between these facts and their manifold meanings. Instead of asking us to advance step by step until we recognize in Jesus, the carpenter's son from Nazareth, the Messiah, the Son of God, John presents us the Christ of faith from the very start. Jesus is the Word of God (1,1), only Son of the Father (1,18); but since the Word became *flesh* (1,14), the object of faith is a human existence in all its historical density—a man who weeps (11,35), feels tired and thirsty (4,6–7), and makes friends (11,5; 13,23). Like that of a great artist, although on a different level, the contemplative outlook of John corresponds to the mystery of the Incarnation, revealing a transparent world, open to eternity.

In the commentaries one can read about the "realized eschatology" that characterizes the fourth gospel. In simpler terms, this means that John gives more weight to the present than to the future: in the life, still more in the death of Jesus, the essential is already present; eternal life begins *right now* in the encounter with Christ (3,16–18; 5,24; 8,51; 17,1–3) although a further fulfillment later on is not denied (e.g. 5,28–29). These different accents should not, however, cause us to forget that a similar concern unites John's reflections and the use of eschatological or apocalyptic categories in the rest of the New Testament: the conviction that in the life and death of Jesus we encounter the decisive turning-point of human history, despite ambiguous or contradictory appearances. The apocalyptic mentality employs the concept of the "end of the world" to describe the true significance of what is happening now (cf. PGod 172–174): the absolute future will reveal the hidden meaning of the present. When the Son of Man comes in glory, everyone will recognize the correctness of Jesus' claims. But we can also invert the terms and say the same thing starting from the other side: to be able to speak in this way about the future, that future must already be operative in some sense today. For John, then, the absolute future is a kind of permanent dimension standing over the entire course of history. It can be called heaven (3,13.31 etc.), the Father's bosom (1,18), his house (14,2). Deeply rooted in this dimension, fully "at home" there, Jesus has this absolute as a constitutive part of his being. He is the *true* light (1,9; cf. 1 John 2,8), the *true* bread from heaven (6,32.55), the *good* shepherd (10,11), the *true* vine (15,1), and so on.

This emphasis on the "already here" does not eliminate the dynamic aspect of this gospel, as one might fear. Here too there is a progression, a road to follow. Jesus is a pilgrim on the way to meet his *hour* that is coming (2,4; 7,30; 8,20; 12,23.27; 13,1; 17.1), the time of the full manifestation of his identity, in biblical language of his *glory*. This definitive hour is "the hour when the Son of Man must be lifted up" (cf. 3,14; 8,28; 12,34), a typically Johannine expression in that it merges both Jesus' death on the cross and his resurrection-ascension, his going up to the Father. An hour that occurs within time and yet which cannot be fully contained within human history, it marks the summit of revelation: "they will look upon the one they have pierced" (19,37; cf. Zech 12,10).

All the New Testament writers testify in one way or another to the fact that in Jesus Christ, the absolute future breaks into our present day. But since John, as we have seen, is especially attentive to this dimension of present fulfillment, for him the problem of its *manifestation* is particularly acute. In other words, if the fulfillment has occurred, how is it that everybody is not aware of it? Here the important question is not "when will all this happen, and what will be the sign that all this is about to come to completion?" (Mark 13,4) but rather "how can we recognize in the life of Jesus signs of God's glory?" Little by little, human beings are divided into those who are able to discern the true identity of Jesus and accept him, and those whose outlook remains superficial, or in John's way of speaking, those born of God and his Spirit, from above (1,13; 3,3.5) and those who belong to the earth (3,31), here below, this world (8,23). It is true that God has sent his Son to save the world (3,16), but in order to receive salvation the world has to reject all self-sufficiency and open itself to something else. To the extent that it wants to be a closed universe with totalitarian pretensions, the world deprives itself of the fullness of life. Those, however, who consent to be reborn of the Spirit (3,5–8), to come with Jesus (1,39), trusting in him (14,1), become capable of understanding and seeing "greater things than these" (1,50). This problematic commands a large part of the fourth gospel, and it is summed up in the prologue: light shines in the world but is not recognized by all;

those who open themselves to it are finally transformed into what they contemplate: born of God, they become fully what they are in reality, children of God (1,9–13; 12,36; cf. 2 Cor 3,18).

The one sent from heaven

After this quick survey of some of the particularities of the gospel according to John, let us now look at how the author presents the way of Jesus. As for other themes, we will find that with respect to the synoptics he radicalizes and systematizes the data, emphasizing especially its deep and permanent significance for the life of faith.

We have seen that, in the other gospels, Jesus is presented as "the One who comes." For his part, John does not hesitate to use this expression to describe Jesus (1,15.27; 3,31), and he is aware that it can be an eschatological or messianic title (6,14; 11,27; 12,13) since the Messiah will "come" (4,25; 7,31.41–42). Already implicit in this title is the fact that the being in question is not a prisoner of this world, of its customs or its values; his roots are elsewhere. John says this explicitly: Jesus is the One-who-comes from above (3,31; cf. 8,23), from heaven (3,31; cf. 3,13; 6,33.41.42.50.51.58; 1 Cor 15,47). In other words, he comes from God (3,2; 8,42; 13,3; 16,27.30; 17,8; cf. 7,29), not from himself (7,28). For John heaven is not, as for us, a vague or even imaginary place, far from the concerns of this earth. It is the dwelling-place of God, or even a synonym of the sacred Name. It thus represents the one true Reality.

The fact that he is thus sent by Another, usually called "the Father" (3,34–35; 6,57; 10,36; cf. 5,43; 12,13) and that he knows it (8,14), makes Jesus a supremely free person. Sure of his indestructible relationship with the Father (8,16b.29), he need not be afraid of human criticisms and judgments (5,34.41), nor need he attempt to justify himself (8,50.54). He can bear witness to himself with no risk of egotism (8,12–18). Paradoxically, the fact that Jesus does not belong to himself, that he has come to do another's will (6,38) and can do (5,19.30) or say (12,49–50) nothing by himself makes him perfectly himself, free and master of his actions. He has not abdicated his liberty by submitting himself to a human being, an idea or an institution that has become an absolute, and thus an idol. On the contrary, he recognizes the truth of his being and lives it out to the full—being the Son of the Father, who is the Source of all life and freedom. Because Jesus does not want to be anything without his Father, with his Father—always there for him (8,29; 16,32)—he is everything: he has received power to give life (5,21; 6,57), to judge (5,22), to do the works of God (5,17.36; 10,25.37–38). In short, the Father has put everything into his hands (13,3a; 3,35). He is thus able to reveal to humanity the ultimate truth about God, his loving designs, and above all the breathtaking beauty of a communion.

If God ("above," "heaven") is thus the starting-point of Jesus' way, what is its end-point? For John, the One-who-comes comes first of all to the *world* (e.g. 6,14; 10,36; 11,27), in other words to the whole of creation culminating in the human race, enjoying a relative autonomy and menaced by the temptation to self-sufficiency. Jesus' coming offers this world, which possesses a certain beauty but is haunted by the sadness of finitude, a way out, the possibility of a better existence. Jesus comes into the world to save it (3,17; 12,47), to bring it life in fullness (10,10; cf. 3,16), to bear witness to the truth that will liberate it (18,37; 8,32). His intention is thus essentially salvific. This is why the image of *light* is often associated with the coming of the Son to the world (1,9; 3,19; 12,46): his presence sheds light on the road, enables people to walk without stumbling, without getting lost (12,35; 11,9–10). In other words, through the life of Jesus God shows us what it means to be fully human ("the truth") and gives us the possibility of living such a life.

Why does John use the image of a descent, a movement from heaven to the world, to describe what will later be called the incarnation of Jesus and its redemptive intent? Some have claimed to see a Platonic or Gnostic model lurking in the background, but before looking for influences from other domains a good methodology requires us to examine the immediate context more closely for possible parallels. And in fact, the notion of God (or his representative) entering into the world is deeply rooted in biblical and apocalyptic literature (PGod 31, 173). As for the Torah, the Law or Word of God, it is sometimes compared to a light (Ps 119,105) because it shows the faithful the right path to take. But the most salient parallel is found in the Wisdom literature of Judaism, the reflection on the pre-existing Divine Wisdom who comes down to earth to enlighten humanity.[1] In Sirach

89

24, for example, God's Wisdom, personified, explains that she had dwelt in heaven before setting out on a pilgrimage through all humanity and finally choosing to settle permanently in Israel:

> I came forth from the mouth of the Most High,
>   and I covered the earth like mist.
> I had my tent in the heights,
>   and my throne was a pillar of cloud.
> Alone, I have made the circuit of the heavens
>   and walked through the depths of the abyss.
> Over the waves of the sea and over the whole earth
>   and over every people and nation I have held sway.
> Among all these I searched for rest,
>   and looked to see in whose territory I might pitch camp.
> Then the Creator of all things instructed me
>   and he who created me fixed a place for my tent.
> He said, "Pitch your tent in Jacob,
>   make Israel your inheritance."
> From eternity, in the beginning, he created me,
>   and for eternity I shall remain.
> In the holy tent I ministered before him
>   and thus became established in Zion.
> In the beloved city he has given me rest,
>   and in Jerusalem I wield my authority.
> I have taken root in a privileged people,
>   in the Lord's property, in his inheritance.
>
>   (Sir 24,3–12 NJB; cf. Prov 8,22–31; Bar 3,32–38)

For the sage, Divine Wisdom present in a more or less hidden way throughout creation is finally recapitulated in the Torah of Moses (Sir 24,22ff; 15,1). Similarly, in the Book of Wisdom, a later work, God sends his Wisdom, present at the creation (Wis 9,9), to lead by her inspiration God's people through all the stages of its history (Wis 9–10). During the Exodus from Egypt, for example, she "guided them by a marvelous road, herself their shelter by day—and their starlight through the night" (10,17 NJB). This meditation on the origins and the activity of Wisdom enabled the thinkers of Israel to link together divine revelation and human reflection, choice of a particular nation and God's presence in creation as a whole, God's transcendence and his activity in the world.

Seen in this context, we can better appreciate the continuity of John's perspective with the entire biblical tradition as well as its element of newness. From the very beginning God has sought to orient and to lead his creation by communicating something of himself, in John's language, by his Word which is life and light (John 1,1–10). This communication occurs in a unique manner in the existence of the people of Israel (1,11a; cf. Sir 24,8.10–12). John shares this outlook with the sages of Israel. But he goes further. For him, the presence of Divine Wisdom in the Torah is not the end of her career, for now she has become fully embodied in a human being: "The Word became flesh and dwelt among us" (1,14). In his meditation on the life of Jesus, John is also more aware of the formidable possibility human beings have of closing their eyes to the light. God does not desire this to happen, of course, but it is nonetheless an aspect of the movement of salvation history. This refusal is visible throughout human history (1,10; cf. Bar 3,15–31) and even in the life of the chosen people (1,11b; cf. Bar 3,1–14; Luke 11,49); it reaches its climax in the crucifixion of God's only Son. In Jesus, God's self-understanding becomes visible and tangible, and walks as a pilgrim along our roads (1,18). From then on, everything depends on our attitude towards him and the consequences we draw from this.

"If you knew what God gives"

In the first three gospels, the activity of the One-who-comes consists in an original teaching about the Reign or Kingdom of God, often by means of parables, and in miraculous acts of healing, gestures that indicate the presence—active but hidden—of the Kingdom. In John's gospel, these two activities are even more united. Jesus performs a few great *signs*, using simple elements of creation—water and wine, bread, light—and transforming them to point to a spiritual reality. To put it another way, the presence of Jesus makes the world transparent so that another dimension can shine through, "heaven" (cf. 1,51). The cosmos is no longer a hermetically sealed world; it has become sacramental. In the acts of Jesus, for those who know how to see, the glory of God shines forth. Jesus' words are often a commentary that brings out the content of the signs. Since the Son *is* the revelation of the Father, all he *does* is revelatory, and he speaks above all to call people's attention to who he is and what he does. If he speaks a great deal about himself and very little about the Kingdom (but cf. 3,3.5), this is because his own existence is the beginning of God's Reign, a portion of the world (of "flesh") that is transfigured, radiant with the glory of God.

The words and acts of Jesus take up the symbols, the institutions and the events of the history of Israel to show their fulfillment. In himself he recapitulates all the gifts God has given to his people throughout the centuries.[2] The water used for the Jewish purifications is transformed into a new and better wine, a symbol of the Kingdom (2,1–12). This first sign recalls the first of the plagues announcing the Exodus from Egypt, the water turned into blood (Ex 7), but here life is the outcome, and not death.[3] Following this, Jesus cleanses the Temple and announces its future rebuilding in three days: he is the true Temple, a meeting-place between God and humanity (2,13–22).

Likewise, the prophets of Israel often speak of the vine as an image of the people of God, carefully cultivated by the Lord in order to bear fruit of righteousness (Isa 5,1–7; Jer 2,21; Ps 80,8ff; Ezek 19,10–14; cf. Ex 15,17); once, Ezekiel even applies the image to the royal family (Ezek 17). Jesus proclaims himself as the true vine, recapitulation of the chosen people and God's special possession in the world (John 15). He is also the good shepherd, the one who gives his life for his sheep, the only one able to lead them towards true life. This image too has a long history in Israel. First applied to God himself (Isa 40,9–11; Ezek 34,7–16; Jer 23,3; Ps 23,1), it was also extended to all the leaders of the people (Jer 2,8; 10,21) starting with David (Ps 78,71) and even Moses (Num 27,17; Isa 63,11; Ps 77,20). By the ministry of these last two men God was truly able to lead his people, whereas others had been bad guides interested only in personal profit (cf. John 10,12, "hired hands"), who preferred to "feed themselves" and had to be replaced by God (Jer 23,1–4; Ezek 34; cf. Zech 11). The image of the shepherd is ideal to indicate the dynamic aspect of a life in the company of God; it recalls the itinerant origins of God's people, the Exodus and the life of the patriarchs.

The great themes of the Exodus, that formative experience of the people of the covenant, are implicitly found throughout John's gospel. The Baptizer describes Jesus as the paschal lamb, slain on the day of liberation (1,29.36; Ex 12). His being lifted up on the cross is compared to the serpent of bronze lifted up by Moses in the desert to heal the sinners who looked upon it (3,14–15; Num 21,4–9; Wis 16,5–12).[4] After the multiplication of the loaves (John 6), Jesus declares that he is the true manna, the bread come from heaven to give life to the world (6,31–33). These words, however, are a trial for the disciples, who *grumble* just as the Israelites in the desert grumbled against Moses and against God (6,41.61; cf. Ex 15,24 etc.; PGod 48, n. 8). Finally the two great symbols of the Feast of Tabernacles, the fountain of water that springs up (7,37–39) and the light that shines on the path (8,12) evoke, in addition to their other overtones, the story of water from the rock (Ex 17,1–7; cf. 1 Cor 10,4) and the pillar of fire that went before the people (Ex 13,21–22). A harvest celebration, the Feast of Tabernacles also commemorated the years of sojourning in the wilderness. A rabbinical tradition speaks of the three great gifts of God during the Exodus: the manna, the water and the pillar of fire. They are each associated with a particular person, Moses, Miriam and Aaron, and according to the tradition, at the death of these three the gifts also disappeared.[5] According to the gospel of John, then, in the coming of Jesus these gifts are more present than ever in the midst of God's people. Jesus is the giver *par excellence,* and the gift; his coming provides human beings with all they need to set out on the road, to live life to the full.[6]

"Come and see"

Jesus is, in fact, the starting-point for a pilgrimage. His coming leads others to come to him. Immediately after the first words of Jesus, Mark had placed the calling of the first disciples: these simple men left home and work to set out on an adventure with the Master. John describes the same process in his own way, by a series of significant verbs. Two disciples of John the Baptist *hear* his testimony in favor of Jesus and *follow* him. Jesus *turns around, looks* at them and asks, "What are you *seeking?*" "Where do you *stay?*" reply the disciples. And Jesus answers, *"Come and see."* They *came* and *saw* where he was *staying* and *stayed* with him (1,35–39). Here we have the disciple's journey in a nutshell. A man or woman listens to the testimony of another believer and begins to set out him- or herself after Jesus until finally there is a personal meeting. To put it another way, the indirect encounter leads to a direct encounter (cf. 4,28–30.39–42). A new stage then begins when the disciple searches and, in the company of Jesus, discovers the source of the Master's activity, the reason for his existence, his "home." Once this has been seen, the disciple can root his or her own life in the same Source. No true understanding of Jesus is possible without running the risk of setting out in his footsteps. Only trust in him will open the door to his identity: "come and you will see."

Those who have made this journey become witnesses in their turn. Andrew *finds* his brother Simon and *brings* him to Jesus. Philip does the same with Nathanael. By his encounter with Jesus, the scepticism of this student of the Torah is turned into faith and Jesus promises him, "You will see better things than this" (1,50). Believers will experience the true identity of Jesus as the link between heaven and earth; here, the eschatological Son of Man appears as the permanent mediator ("stairway, ladder," cf. Gen 28,12) between humanity and God (1,51).

This general framework of discipleship does not take all the possibilities into account. People come to Jesus in all sorts of ways: a prominent man visits him secretly at night (3,2), a Samaritan woman meets him while going to the well to draw water (4,7), some women friends of his come out to greet him (11,20.29), crowds flock to him on account of the miraculous signs he performs (6,5.24; 10,41; 11,45; 12,9.11.18–19) and at a critical moment even some non-Jews try to catch a glimpse of him (12,20–21). All these undertakings are not equivalent: even if "everybody" goes toward Jesus (3,26; 12,19), John is well aware that often they are motivated by a superficial, self-seeking faith, more concerned with their own personal or collective advantages than with the risk of trusting (2,23–25). Certainly, Jesus is the source of life in its fullness (10,10) and he rejects no one (6,37b). Those who come to him will no longer be hungry (6,35), the thirsty will always find something to drink (7,37–38) and the blind will recover their sight (9,7)—in short, people are right to come to him to have light (8,12) and life (5,40). But the road to life is Jesus himself (14,6) and following him means continuing to advance even when one no longer understands (6,60–69). Whoever wants to welcome what Jesus has to offer must be ready to let themselves be transformed heart and soul by the gift. In this sense it is more difficult to receive than to give, for the act of receiving requires a letting go, a surrender of one's own autonomy in order to become a pilgrim with Jesus.

In chapter 6 we discover step by step, by the use of the symbol of bread, all the consequences of welcoming Jesus' gift. The chapter begins with the account of the multiplication of the loaves, a story told by all the evangelists. For the others, the miracle of the loaves and fishes is above all a sign of the over-flowing generosity of God shown in Jesus, whereas for John it is used as the first stage of a development of the whole idea of giving and receiving. Those who benefit from this sign remain at first on a superficial level, the level of material advantages. They want to force Jesus to become their king (6,15) and they continue to follow him in the hope of filling their stomachs once more with bread (6,22–26). For his part Jesus tries to make them reach a deeper level: "Work not for perishable food but for food that remains to eternal life, food which the Son of Man will give you" (6,27a).

Then, Jesus explains to them that material bread is only a sign of something else. The true bread from heaven, the essential gift of God that gives life to the world, is Jesus himself (6,32–35). And he continues:

> Truly I tell you,
> unless you eat the flesh of the Son of Man
> and drink his blood,
> you will not have life in you.
> Whoever eats my flesh and drinks my blood
> has eternal life,
> and I will raise him up on the last day. (6,53–54)

The crudity of these words shock some of his disciples, and from then on "they cease to follow him" (6,66). They take his words too literally, when in fact they are "spirit . . . and life" (6,63). Can we not see, however, behind this refusal to dirty their hands, a deeper motivation: the fear of accepting a gift that would unsettle too much their own world-view, that would set them adrift on the high seas with no other landmark or security than Jesus himself (cf. 6,16–21)? We are quite happy with a teacher who tells us interesting things about God, a miracle-worker who distributes food at mealtime, but watch out if he wants to give us too much! Untimely presents will only make our life more complicated. The new wine will undoubtedly cause the wineskins to burst.

Consequently, to follow Jesus we need a hunger and a thirst big enough for what he wants to give us. And this desire can only be awakened in us by God himself. The disciple then discovers at a given moment that his decision to come, motivated by a number of human factors that are more or less imperfect, was in reality obedience to a secret call coming straight from the Source: "All that the Father gives me will come to me . . . no one can come to me unless the Father who sent me draws him . . . everyone who has listened to the Father and learns from him comes to me . . . no one can come to me unless it has been given to him by the Father" (6,37.44.45.65). This is nothing other than a new birth, from above (3,3–8), a birth not of the flesh but of God (1,13). The essential does not consist in a human activity but in the willingness to follow, to trust, to let oneself be born of God. To those who ask, "What must we do to do the works of God?" Jesus replies, "The work of God is that you believe in the one he sent" (6,28–29). As with the Samaritan woman, Jesus seems to make demands upon our good will, our desire to *act well* ("Give me to drink" 4,7), but the further we go, the more we discover that it is not so much a question of giving as of *receiving* (4,10), and that this commits us far more than a passing act of kindness that would leave our illusory autonomy intact.

The crisis of the world

The offer of life in fullness, the glory of God present in the world through the coming of the Son, exercises a power of attraction that creates communion. And yet there are those who do not come (5,40), or who leave the road after they are underway (6,66; cf. 13,30). Gradually, the hearers separate into two camps as a consequence of their basic attitude toward Jesus. Are they ready or not to accept the gift? The answer to this question will reveal the depths of their heart; the choice for or against Jesus is, in the final analysis, equivalent to a choice for or against life and light.

The expression John uses to indicate this separation is the word *krisis*, "judgment." Once again, the evangelist borrows an eschatological expression and shows its relevance to the present day. The important thing is not a judgment exercised by God "at the end of time" but accepting and trusting in Jesus and his message *today* (3,18; 5,24). True, Jesus has come to save, not to judge (3,17; 8,15; 12,47); his intention is to give freely (1,12; 4,10; 7,37), to welcome all who come (6,37b; cf. 12,32). But since in him the Father has given everything without eliminating human freedom, there remains the possibility of refusing the salvation that is offered. The coming of the Son thus places human beings before a fundamental alternative. It is a "crisis" that leads to a division (7,43; 10,19); it calls into question the apparent order of things (9,39; 15,22).

The first part of John's gospel (ch. 1–12) thus takes the form of a great trial. People give or listen to testimony concerning Jesus, but in fact they themselves are "judged." On the one hand there are those who do not welcome the gift of God. They cling to appearances (7,24); they judge in a superficial manner (8,15) and do not penetrate, like Jesus, to the underlying reality by a judgment that is right (5,30; 7,24) and true (8,16). They seek prestige and honor in the eyes of others (5,44; 12,43) and are afraid of being looked down upon (12,42). They remain passionately attached to their habits and privileges without attempting to discover the deeper meaning of these (5,39–40; 8,33). In short, they flee the light (3,19–20). They do not want to come to Jesus to have life (5,40) and "on the last day" that will become evident (12,48; 5,29).

Others are able to receive from Jesus "words of eternal life" (6,68). They come to him and see; they listen to his voice and trust in him. They remain with him, even though they do not always understand the significance of his words and deeds. In this way they show that they are "born of God" (1,13), given to Jesus by the Father (6,37.39; 10,29; 17,2.6.9.11.24). These people have no judgment to fear (3,18) since it is already behind them: in the company of Jesus they have passed over from death to life (5,24) and in the end this too will be evident (5,29).

To appreciate correctly the meaning of these affirmations, it is essential to situate them in the basic perspective of Saint John instead of interpreting them according to our own modern mentality. The fourth gospel is not a sociological study of life in Palestine at the beginning of our age. The author does not intend to affirm, for example, that all those who were unwilling or unable to recognize Jesus as the Messiah of Israel were (or are) guilty of a sin against the light. John does not share our modern interest in subjectivity, nor in historical and sociocultural conditioning. He simply wants us to understand that in Jesus of Nazareth, the itinerant preacher of two thousand years ago, we are in fact confronted with the deepest meaning of our life. In Jesus Christ, the end-point of our searching, our true happiness, the reason we were created, enters fully into human history. His life and message are and will remain the ultimate standard by which our existence will be measured, even if we do not know this yet. For this reason, the choice for or against him, with all that this implies, is the only true alternative appearing in countless shapes and sizes in the history of the universe. Objectively, regardless of our subjective understanding, Jesus is the last word God has to say, and consequently he is our absolute future.

Once this is grasped, we must immediately add that John integrates the subjective dimension in his own fashion. Although in one sense everything is given from the very beginning of this gospel, the author shows in different ways how this "already given" becomes more and more manifest and is better assimilated. The process resembles less a linear progression than the creation of a painting by an artist by means of successive brushstrokes. At the beginning of the gospel, the great Johannine themes such as "life," "glory," and "judgment" are evoked in an indeterminate, global manner, and in successive chapters they appear in an increasingly more nuanced way.

In John 3,35, for instance, Jesus declares, "The Father loves the Son and has given all things in his hand." Later on this "all" is explained: the Father has given the Son the power to judge, which for John, as we have seen, consists mainly in the ability to give life (5,19–30). Then we learn that the Son exercises this power by becoming food for the faithful; he gives his life so that we can enter into the same relationship he has with the Father (6,57). In chapter 8, in a climate of hostility, Jesus states that he benefits from the constant support of the Father and that for his part he always does what pleases the Father, whereas his opponents do not know the Father (vv. 27–29.42–44.54–55). All this leads to the majestic affirmation of Jesus that closes the circle: "I and the Father are one" (10,30.38). At the end of this progression, these simple words are full of meaning for the listener, and this meaning becomes even deeper later on with the raising of

Lazarus (11,41–42), the voice from heaven (12,28) and especially Jesus' prayer on the eve of his death (ch. 17).[7]

As in the other gospels, then, John gives us a progressive revelation of Jesus' identity and his mission. It is not a matter of "all or nothing," right from the start. Some people follow him and enter ever more deeply into his mystery, while others grow in opposition to him. What was once mere incomprehension turns into the active desire to get rid of the troublemaker.

For John, the end of this progressive revelation of Jesus is his *hour*, a much more complex reality than a simple number on a calendar or on the face of a clock. First of all, it is an hour that *comes* (2,4; 7,30; 8,20; 12,23; 13,1; 17,1; cf. 4,21; 5,28; 7,6), an hour determined only by the will of the Father.[8] It must not be confused with our earthly reckoning of time: even though for Jesus it is identified with the gift of his life on the cross (e.g. 12,23ff), it is not limited to one moment of history but dilates until it encounters every human being in their own day. "The hour is coming and is now" (4,23; 5,25), in the encounter with the Son. It is the hour of the full manifestation of his identity, in Johannine language of his glorification (12,23; cf. 7,39), when the true meaning of our choices for or against the light will become visible (cf. 19,37).

A paradoxical ascent

The hour of Jesus is above all "the hour to cross over from this world to the Father" (13,1). Whereas the first part of John's gospel describes the pilgrimage of the one who comes from heaven into the world to save it, the second part (beginning with ch. 13) is centered on the departure of Jesus, his ascent to go back "where he was before" (6,62). John emphasizes the fact that this departure is neither the downfall of Jesus and the triumph of his enemies nor the abandonment of his disciples, but the fulfillment of his mission by the creation of a new road that joins God and humanity in a lasting communion.

Already in his dialogue with Nicodemus, Jesus had spoken of an *ascent* or *going up* to heaven (3,13; cf. 6,62). In the same breath he mentions an image taken from the book of Exodus: "Just as Moses lifted up the serpent in the wilderness, so the Son of Man must be lifted up" (3,14; cf. Num 21,4–9). The final phrase is a passive construction: something is done to Jesus by others. In addition, we find the "must" (*dei*) that so often in the gospels is used to evoke the sovereign will of the Father, the basic motivating force of human history.[9] Later on, we learn that the "Jews" who do not understand him are going to lift him up (8,28) and still later, John explains that this lifting up refers to his imminent death on the cross (12,33; cf. 18,32). And each time the act is shown to have a salvific intent: Jesus will be lifted up to give those who believe eternal life (3,15), to reveal his true identity as God's only Son (8,28), and to create a universal communion around him (12,32).[10]

Elsewhere, Jesus speaks instead of his *departure*, his *going away*. He is going away to the one who sent him, where his enemies will not be able to touch him (7,33–34; 8,21), where even his disciples will not be able to follow him at once (13,33.36). The synoptic gospels, it should be remembered, conclude with a long journey to Jerusalem. In John's gospel, twice the departure or ascent to the Father is implicitly identified with the pilgrimage to Jerusalem. In chapter 7, Jesus' kinsmen challenge him to go up to Jerusalem during the Feast of Tabernacles to manifest himself openly. Aware of the hostility towards him and knowing that his hour has not yet come, Jesus refuses, making the journey later in secret. And in chapter 11, Jesus decides with full awareness, in spite of the growing opposition against him and at the risk of his life, to go into Judea (v. 8) the third day (v. 6) to raise his friend Lazarus from death (vv. 6–16). Much more than a simple journey to the capital for a religious festival, the pilgrimage to Jerusalem is for Jesus an encounter with his hour, a going away and a going up to the Father.

After the raising of Lazarus, the final and greatest sign performed by Jesus during his itinerant ministry, the hostility against him reaches its highest point and he withdraws once again (11,53–54). Nevertheless, as the feast of Passover approaches Jesus, ready for death (12,1–8), makes his solemn entry into the Holy City like the poor king predicted by the prophets, followed by the whole world (12,12–19). Earlier Jesus had refused to be acclaimed as a king by the crowd (6,15). But now, at the end of his life, when all ambiguity is removed, this theme will suddenly come into prominence.

The end of chapter 12 clearly links the two paradoxical dimensions of Jesus' elevation. The coming of some non-Jews eager to see Jesus is for him the sign that his hour has finally come, since the prophecies of the Gentiles coming up to the Holy City are now being fulfilled (cf. Isa 2,2–4; PGod 125–126, 135–136, 154–155, 161–162). This is the hour of the *glorification* of the Son of Man (12,23), the definitive revelation of his identity as Son of the Father. But it is likewise the hour of his abasement, like the seed that falls into the ground to die (12,24). Jesus both looks forward to and fears this paradoxical hour. He experiences a moment of inner debate analogous to the struggle in Gethsemani described by the synoptics before emerging victorious, strengthened by his trust in the Father (12,27ff). What seems a failure in human eyes is in fact the founding of a reconciled humanity (12,32).

At this critical juncture, Jesus explains more clearly what is involved in a disciple's calling. Coming to him is only the first step: after this, he has to be *followed* in his act of self-surrender which is the road toward the Father (12,26). The bystanders cannot understand this; for them the Messiah must "remain forever" (12,34). "The crowd" prefers tranquil possession to the hardships of a pilgrimage. Since they do not want to set out on the road, following the light, they condemn themselves to remain in the darkness (12,35), stumbling like blind people (cf. 12,40), while Jesus passes on (12,36). For them the ascent of Jesus is merely his disappearance, the tragic though predictable end of his career.

The first part of John's gospel concludes with a portrait of Jesus offering life in fullness to his contemporaries one last time. They refuse to follow him, "for they loved the glory of men more than the glory of God" (12,43; cf. 5.44). In this way they unwittingly transform the good news of salvation into a standard to measure their conduct (12,46–48). Henceforth, Jesus leaves them alone and spends the last days of his life on earth with the small community of his disciples, those whom the Father gave him to continue his work in the world.

The road to the Father

With chapter 13 we enter upon the hour of Jesus, his passing over to the Father which coincides with the Jewish Passover

(13,1). Because of its great density of meaning this stage occupies in the gospel a place out of all proportion to its chronological duration: seven chapters (13–19), in other words more than a fourth of the gospel, to recount a period of less than twenty-four hours. In the synoptic gospels, the events of the passion and death of Jesus are preceded by the account of the last supper when, by his acts and words during the meal, Jesus expresses the meaning of his imminent death. John goes further in this direction, describing a symbolic act of Jesus and then explaining it: Jesus' words turn into a long discourse-dialogue with the disciples that is then recapitulated in a prayer to the Father. The whole thing (ch. 13–17) is generally called the last or farewell discourse. It represents Jesus' last will and testament, a charter for the constitution of the community that will continue his mission after his departure to the Father.

First of all, there is the eloquent gesture by which Jesus shows who he is by revealing the deepest meaning of his coming and his going away. Here we do not witness the transformation of bread and wine into his body broken and his blood spilt, but the significance is of the same order. Jesus takes off his garments and washes the feet of his disciples. In taking the place of a slave or of someone who wants to honor deeply another person, Jesus, the Lord and Master, performs a mind-boggling reversal of the customary order of things. This is an act of service, of cleansing, and perhaps still more of tenderness. In short, it is a revelation of the ultimate meaning of love (13,1) which will be fulfilled the following day on the cross—a love which is divine and not human in its origin, but has become human in and through the life of the Son.

In revealing his secret in this way, Jesus acts from a place inaccessible to human beings and overturns all our earthly categories. For this reason, in order to imitate him, to "follow" him, the disciples must first receive the ability to do this from their Teacher. In symbolic terms, they must allow him to wash their feet. Peter cannot understand this: he reacts by a refusal that suddenly turns into its opposite (13,6–9), a misguided generosity that tries to go ahead too quickly and so becomes presumptuous (13,36–38). His relationship with his Teacher is still too human. He still depends too much on his own understanding of Jesus, on his own ability to follow him. In the final analysis,

Peter wants to lead his own life; he does not yet see the need to surrender himself, to receive.

In other words, Peter and his companions are fundamentally incapable of grasping the real reason for the departure of Jesus in order to accomplish his mission, a departure that will enable them to follow him along the road of service and love, the road to the Father. Without this act of self-giving to the end, to death, God's love would not be totally incarnate in human history. It would remain an abstraction for us, an ideal or aspiration with no guarantee that it would ever come about. If, however, Jesus washes his disciples' feet by lowering himself out of love for them, then they in turn will be able to do this for one another. They will have an example to follow (13,15) and will be sent out in their turn (13,16.20). The ascent of Jesus, in other words his descent out of love, is the only way to break the glass of a world closed in upon itself in narcissistic self-contemplation and to open a road of communion with the Father.

If this is the case, then it implies in addition that Jesus' execution, the ultimate manifestation of the power of evil (13,2.27; cf. 8,44), contributes paradoxically, on a deeper level, to the realization of God's plan. It becomes the means for Jesus to be lifted up, to go away in order to open the way to the Father. In other words, Satan cooperates, unknowingly and unintentionally, in the saving work of God. John is perhaps the gospel writer most aware of this fact so difficult to express without distorting it, which explains the great use he makes of irony here.

This irony is visible for example in the words of the high priest, much more significant than their explicit intention: "It is in your interest that one person should die for the people instead of the whole nation perishing" (11,50). Similarly, in his presentation of Judas, John shows us to what extent the love of the Son neutralizes the spirit of evil. Jesus knows "from the beginning" who will betray him (6,64.70–71; 13,11.18), and yet he keeps him in his inner circle and, at the very moment Judas is preparing to hand him over, gives him a further sign of his preference by sharing a bit of food with him (13,26).[11] The following words make a surprising link between this gesture of friendship and the hostile intention of Judas: "And after the morsel of food, Satan entered into him. Jesus therefore said to him, 'What you are doing, do it quickly'" (13,27). It would be erroneous to conclude from this that Jesus and Satan have similar outlooks or designs, or that the deed of Judas, who leaves the light for the darkness outside (13,30), is in any way justified. Jesus is "upset" (13,21), wounded by the infidelity of one of his closest associates, but it is precisely his acceptance of this suffering and his gift of love in return that "disarm" Satan and enroll him in the service of life. No victory over the formidable forces of evil is possible by using the same weapons. Only a love that forgives and that consents to suffer can defeat death from within by transfiguring it into the road to life.

After the departure of Judas, which sets in motion the forces of destruction, Jesus begins his last conversation with his disciples. The parallels between these chapters and the Book of Deuteronomy have often been noted.[12] In both cases we have a farewell discourse pronounced by leaders, Moses or Jesus, about to leave their followers. The leader speaks words of encouragement and comfort in light of the fact that he will soon be absent, as well as proferring instructions for the future life of the group, the relations among its members and towards their adversaries. The basic purpose of the discourse is to help the hearers to stay together, faithful to their common roots. In other words, it has the same role as the charter of a covenant. Deuteronomy recalls the miracle of the Exodus and the journey in the desert, emphasizing the formation of the people by the free and undeserved choice of the Lord (e.g. Deut 7,7–8; 9,5–6). It exhorts the faithful to keep on walking along the ways of God by keeping his commandments, in order to receive their rest and the constant presence of the Lord in their midst. The faithful, in turn, must transmit these words to future generations. In this way a nation is born and becomes, in human history, a living sign of the existence and the identity of the God of Israel.

John, for his part, does not speak explicitly of a covenant. But it would not be incorrect to see in the farewell discourse a commentary on the "new covenant" (Luke 22,20; cf. Jer 31,31) that Jesus founds by his passover to the Father.[13] The disciples have to understand that their Master's departure to a place to which they cannot yet go (13,33) is necessary, and even salutary, because it is the prelude to a new form of presence, deeper and more lasting. This going away is the other side of a coming that institutes a new and universal communion; by it Jesus bestows the gift of brotherly love, the existential sign of God's presence at the heart of the world. Already for the people of the Exodus, the Law was first and foremost a *gift* of God that ratified his covenant and turned them into the people of God. Here, the "new commandment" is even more clearly a gift and not an order, since it cannot be put into practice by any merely human effort, however great. If it is in fact being lived out, that means that God in person is present and active.

Jesus tries to explain the meaning of his coming departure in different ways. He is going to prepare a place for his disciples in his Father's house, before coming to take them with him. He is, in fact, the way to the Father (14,2–6). His departure thus permits the creation of a relationship of perfect communion between humanity and God (cf. 1,51). On account of his going away and his presence with the Father, the disciples will be able to do the works of Jesus and even "greater ones than these" (14,12); they will go in their turn and bear much fruit.

Jesus' ascent to the Father will bring about a new form of presence: "I will not leave you orphans; I am coming to you" (14,18). In other words, Jesus will ask the Father to send "another Paraclete" (14,16) to be with them for ever. The word "paraclete" means "support, defender, comforter"; its primary meaning is juridical, the attorney who defends the accused man or woman. Here it indicates God's active and effective presence in the midst of the community of disciples, their faithful support amidst the trials of existence in a hostile world. This "other Paraclete" is immediately identified with the Spirit who will keep the disciples in the truth of Jesus (14,17), and a short while later Jesus explains how this will come about (16,13): the Spirit will lead the faithful along the road of the fullness of truth, Jesus' road, the road which *is* Jesus (cf. 14,6). This ascending and active movement, however, is balanced by its counterpart, a descending movement, since we must never forget that we are dealing first and foremost with a gift from God: the Spirit comes "to announce the things to come" (*ta erchomena*). By the use of this expression with apocalyptic overtones, John discreetly indicates that the truth in question is the full revelation of God's plan.[14] The Spirit will make sure that the message of Jesus never becomes a dead letter but remains constantly alive and a source of life (14,26). Strengthened by his presence, the disciples will bear witness to their Lord (15,26–27) and will thus confound a world sure that it had brought this "Jesus business" to an end (16,8).

This coming of the Spirit (15,26; 16,13) does not exclude or replace the coming of Jesus himself. Jesus is coming to his own (14,3.18), coming with the Father to those who love him to make his home with them (14,23). The coming of Jesus in the first part of the gospel was a coming into the world to save it; this coming is a coming to those who keep his word. They will see him, but the world will not see him any longer (14,19; cf. Heb 9,28). It is a coming that is the fruit of an absence: "I am going away and I am coming to you" (14,28).[15]

Henceforth, what is most important for the disciples is to remain in Jesus like the branches on the vine, in order to bear fruit (15,1–8). The true vine, image of God's people, is Jesus; it is also Jesus together with those who belong to him. Jesus and the community of disciples are not two separate realities, for this community exists only insofar as it is "in him." Remaining in Jesus means keeping his commandments (15,10), notably the commandment to love one's brothers and sisters (15,12), to give one's life (15,13). It also means being a friend of Jesus, not just a slave or a servant (15,14–15) but someone who knows full well what he or she is doing, who has a direct relationship with the Father (16,26–27; 20,17). The life of the disciples will not be easy; they will experience opposition and even hostility from a world that put to death their Master (15,18—16,4). Nonetheless, in the full assurance that in Jesus the love of God has made ultimately powerless a hostile world (16,33), their lives will be characterized by unshakeable peace (16,33a; 14,27) and joy (15,11; 16,20–24; 17,13).

It is evident that, at the last supper, the disciples are not able to grasp all this. And yet Jesus wants to say it, since he has his eyes on the future. Three separate times he states: "I have told you this now before it happens, so that when it does happen you will believe" (14,29; 13,19; 16,4). At present, at the end of a long spiritual journey, the disciples are finally able to believe that their Master "has come out from God" (16,30), but everything that has to do with his departure, its necessity and its meaning, still remains incomprehensible to them.[16] To understand it, they will have to undergo another enlightenment, a consequence of the resurrection (cf. 20,17b). At present, they do not yet see the need to be washed by Jesus (13,7) nor do they grasp what is going on between him and Judas (13,22.28–29). At first, they cannot understand that Jesus is going to leave them to go to a place where they cannot follow (13,37). Then later, when they do realize this, the only result is that they are deeply troubled (14,1.27; 16,6.20–22). Thomas sums up well their present frame of mind when he says, "Lord, we don't know where you are going. How can we know the way?" (14,5). Before the coming of the Spirit, a consequence of Jesus' departure, any reference to this departure and its meaning strikes the disciples as pure gibberish, a foreign tongue they do not yet understand (16,5–6.16–18). Blinded by the sorrow of the approaching hour, the hour of separation and of scattering (16,21.32), the disciples are unable to bear the whole truth (16,12). Even the faith they have acquired will not resist the trial of the hour: Jesus knows ahead of time that he will be abandoned by everyone, left alone to face his future (16,31–32).

Both the way of Jesus and that of his disciples thus pass through the experience of separation, of painful solitude in order to make possible a fullness of communion. That is why, before leaving his companions, Jesus speaks words of comfort to them. It is also why he concludes his farewell speech with the great prayer of chapter 17. Jesus, on his way to the Father (vv. 11,13), remembers his disciples still in the world and asks that they may be part of the same relationship of communion uniting the Father and the Son. In this way they will be protected against the forces of dispersion and destruction; their unity in love will be the sign that they are not prisoners of a world doomed to death but that in them the life-giving presence of Jesus and his Father remains active.

While thus being "with Jesus" (v. 24), the disciples from now on are called to be *in* the world (vv. 11,15) without being *of* the world (vv. 14,16). They are sent out, exactly in the same manner that Jesus himself was sent by the Father (v. 18). If Jesus no longer seems interested in the world in general (v. 9), that is not because it has now been definitively rejected or condemned. On the contrary, the object of Jesus' mission remains that "the world may believe" (v. 21) and recognize in Jesus the one sent by God (v. 23). But from now on, this purpose will be accomplished through the existence of the disciples and those who will follow in their footsteps (v. 20), the community of believers down through the ages, what we call the Church. Through the existence of this community, by its unity with the Father and the Son and among its members, Jesus and his work remain present in human history. In it the glory of God (v.22), his radiant love (v. 26), shines in the darkness of the world (cf. 1,5).

"Here is your King!"

In his account of the Passion, John follows the other gospels much more closely than in the rest of his work. At the same time he eliminates or downplays elements of hesitation and humiliation in the behavior of Jesus such as the agony in Gethsemani, the mockery of the bystanders under the cross and the final cry of abandonment. John emphasizes all that shows Jesus, even in his extreme abasement, as fully master of the situation. Jesus in fact is in charge; he gives himself consciously and deliberately (cf 10,18). In a word, Jesus is the *king*, although in a completely different way than the rulers of this world whose authority is based on constraint (18,36). Jesus' authority flows naturally from his identity as Son of God: when he is arrested he has merely to reveal this identity by using the expression "I am" (18,6; cf. 8,24.28; 13,19) to prompt an instinctive movement of homage, or even of adoration, from his adversaries.[17]

Jesus' kingship reflects the truth of his being (18,37). It consists in the fact that he is the good shepherd (10,11), the only Son sent by the Father into the world to lead human beings towards true life. There is no way Jesus can lose this kind of kingship. He has no need to cling to it jealously, to attempt to compete with Caesar, for example. He is king simply by being true to himself. This is the source of the gospel paradox: Jesus is never more clearly a king than when he is utterly destitute and powerless, when, bereft of all human comeliness, he gives himself freely to open a way between humanity and the Father. The downward movement is therefore in reality an upward movement. For this reason, John views as extremely significant the fact that Jesus dies on a cross in the Roman fashion and not by stoning, the Jewish method (18,31–32). This is also the reason why the evangelist emphasizes so strongly the notice nailed to the cross giving the reason for his condemnation, a classic example of Johannine irony: the crucified Jesus is proclaimed universal king by an inscription in three languages.

In John's gospel, the passion of Jesus is a long reflection on authentic power and authority. It takes the form of a trial where

Jesus is condemned to death for his claims to royalty and to divinity, but in fact in the encounter with Jesus the others are the ones who are judged, their true intentions and motives unveiled. Peter is afraid and denies any relationship with him (18,17.25–27). The Jewish leaders proclaim, "We have no king but Caesar!" (19,15). In this way these men, so careful about their ritual purity (18,28) and eager to find Jesus guilty of blasphemy (19,7), in the end commit the greatest blasphemy of all.

The central figure who stands before Jesus during his trial is the Roman governor, Pontius Pilate. In his case too the irony is manifest. An imposing representative of the almighty occupying power, imperial Rome, he is little by little reduced to utter impotence when confronted with this condemned man who seems so utterly alone and helpless. Pilate is already made ridiculous by the very choreography of the trial. Forced to run back and forth between the "pure" Jews outside the palace and the prisoner inside with the pagans, he resembles more closely a courtier than a ruler. Convinced of Jesus' innocence, he is unable to save him from death. The impressive Roman system of justice is ultimately shown to be powerless to bring about justice. The theme of truth is a stumbling-block for Pilate, and at the end he remains alone with his two questions, which must now remain unanswered: "What is truth?" (18,38) and "Where are you from?" (19,9). All he can do, and without intending to, is to proclaim to the world Jesus' identity: the One who is fully human (19,5), the King (19,14; cf. 19,19ff).

When the condemnation is finally decided upon, Jesus himself takes charge of things. He carries his cross alone (no mention here of the Cyrenian!) and *goes out* to the place of his execution (19,17). John insists strongly on Jesus' death as a *fulfillment* of God's plan: "aware that everything was already fulfilled, so that Scripture might be fulfilled ... Jesus said, 'It is fulfilled'" (19,28–30). Compared to the rest of the fourth gospel, the biblical quotations and allusions are quite numerous here. The paschal symbolism especially is very clear: Jesus dies at the hour when, in the Temple, the lambs are being killed for the Passover meal (19,14) and, like the lambs, his bones must not be broken (19,36; cf Ex 12,46). There are also allusions to the persecuted righteous man of the Psalms (garments divided up Ps 22,18; thirst Ps 22,15; 69,21; bones Ps 34,20) and the Pierced One of Second Zechariah (19,37; cf. Zech 12,10; PGod 179). Once again, the important thing for John is not Jesus' death, but his giving of his life. He is active, in other words able to give life, even at the time of greatest passivity in a human existence, death. "Bowing his head, he handed over the spirit" (19,30). With a typically Johannine play on words, the evangelist indicates that for Jesus, death is nothing other than communicating the breath of life to others. There is also that curious detail to which John accords such great importance—the blood and water that flow from Jesus' side after he has been struck by the spear (19,34–35). The same idea is at work here: the death of Jesus is in reality the gushing forth of new life, the giving of the Spirit. The road down to death is in fact a pilgrimage up to the Father to open a new way, a departure to make possible a new and a life-giving coming: "I am going away and I am coming to you . . . it is in your interest that I go away, for if I do not go away, the Paraclete will not come to you" (14,28; 16,7).

In our study of the synoptic gospels, we distinguished in the way of Jesus two stages: first an itinerant ministry in the towns and countrysides of Galilee, then a pilgrimage up to Jerusalem (developed in greatest detail by Luke), the place of his Passover, his death and resurrection. John takes up these two stages in his own fashion, transposing them to another level. Jesus expresses this in a phrase full of meaning spoken just before his death: "I came from the Father and I have come into the world; now I am leaving the world and journeying to the Father" (16,28). Jesus knows "that he has come from God and that he is going away to God" (13,3).[18]

Having come into the world to save it by offering it true life, Jesus realizes that the world as a whole does not want to listen to him, although some people "born of God" do come and stay with him (cf. 1,10–12). Jesus comes so that women and men can come to him: this is the result of the first half of the gospel. He is "the Christ, the Son of God, the One-who-comes into the world" (11,27).

The second half of the gospel is centered on the departure of Jesus by means of his death on the cross. This departure seems to be the result of a failure, the triumph of evil. In fact, this hour of darkness (cf. 9,4; 13,30) is the hour of a new birth (16,21; cf.

3,3–5). Jesus goes away so that his disciples can follow him, so that they can enter into his communion with the Father (13,36; 14,3) and come into the world in their turn as witnesses to this communion (17,17–23) or, in John's language, to be consecrated and sent forth. By his ascent to the Father, an ascent that in no way annuls his coming, Jesus shows that he is the *Way* (14,6) henceforth open between the world and the Father. The historical events of Jesus' life and death thus acquire a permanent, "transhistorical" dimension. An opening has been made for all time in the veil separating human beings from God (cf. Mark 15,38; Heb 6,19–20; 9,11–12.24; 10,20).

The establishment of this ladder or staircase between earth and heaven (cf. 1,51) is a consequence of Jesus' being lifted up on the cross, a fruit of the seed that fell into the ground (12,24). But this fruit remains hidden from the disciples until his coming at Easter (20,19) to begin the first Day of a new week. In the meantime, the King reposes in his perfumed garden (19,38–42; cf. Song of Songs 4,12ff). The universe implodes into an Eden from which life can spring forth once again.

Questions for Reflection

1. According to John, the Son comes into the world to give life in all its fullness (cf. John 3,16–17; 10,10). What does the expression "life in fullness" suggest to me? Where can this life be found? What obstacles keep me from attaining it?

2. In himself, Jesus recapitulates all the gifts God has given to his people throughout the centuries. In this respect, what is the significance of the images of bread (John 6), of the shepherd (John 10), of the vine (John 15), of light (John 1,9; 3,19; 8,12; 11,9f; 12,35–46) that John applies to Jesus?

3. For John, judgment (*krisis*) is not essentially an act that takes place at the end of time but the basic alternative set before us by the coming of Christ into the world. The coming of the light leads to a choice that has to be repeated over and over again: running towards or running away, trusting or attempting to justify oneself, welcoming the gift or remaining self-sufficient. By what kinds of alternatives does this judgment work itself out concretely in my life today? How can we understand Jesus' words when he says that in his company we have already passed over from death to life (John 5,24)?

111

4. Jesus' departure, far from being the proof of his failure, is the fulfill-ment of his mission. His descent out of love is in reality an ascent to the Father to open a way for us, to establish an unbreakable commun-ion between humanity and God. How does the episode of the washing of the disciples' feet (John 13) illustrate these statements? Why does Jesus say, "If I do not wash you, you will have no part with me . . . A servant is not greater than his master, nor is a messenger greater than the one who sent him" (John 13,8.16)?

5. How does Jesus' relationship with Judas, and the way he treats his betrayer (see especially John 13,21–30) help us to understand better his life and his message?

6. The passion of Jesus according to John is, among other things, a meditation on the kingship of Jesus. What does it tell us about true authority, its source, its significance and its purpose?

Notes

[1]Cf. Raymond E. Brown, *The Gospel according to John I-XII* (Garden City, NY: Doubleday, 2nd ed. 1977), "Wisdom Motifs," pp. cxxii-cxxv.

[2]Cf. Jacques Guillet, *Entre Jésus et l'Eglise* (Paris: Seuil, 1985), pp. 287–288.

[3]Cf. T. Francis Glasson, *Moses in the Fourth Gospel* (London: SCM Press, 1963), p. 26.

[4]Glasson, pp. 33–34, mentions another parallel. The expression used by John to speak of the two men crucified with Jesus in 19,18, "one on either side," seems to be an allusion to Ex 17,12, where Aaron and Hur, standing on either side of Moses on top of a hill, hold up his arms until sunset to ensure victory for the Israelites. Furthermore, in the rabbinical writings, it seems that this story is combined with the bronze serpent lifted up by Moses in the desert. It is worth noting in this respect that John does not call the men crucified with Jesus "rob-bers" (Mark, Matthew) or "criminals" (Luke), nor does he mention their insulting Jesus (cf. Mark 15,32b).

[5]Glasson, pp. 60–64.

[6]We should also mention in passing the relationship between John 14,2 ("I am going to prepare you a place") and Deut 1,33, where we read that God "went ahead of you on your journey . . . to search out places for you to camp." The gospel text is even closer to the Targums than to the literal text of Deuteronomy. See Ignace de la Potterie, *La vérité dans saint Jean. Tome I: Le Christ et la vérité; l'Esprit et la vérité* (Rome: Biblical Institute Press, 1977), pp. 250–251. Regarding parallels be-tween the Exodus and the gospel according to John see also F.-M.

Braun, *Jean le Théologien. II: Les grandes traditions d'Israel et l'accord des écritures d'après le quatrième évangile* (Paris: Gabalda, 1964), pp. 187–206; Donatien Mollat, *Etudes johanniques* (Paris: Seuil, 1979), pp. 17–23.

[7]Cf. C.H. Dodd, *The Interpretation of the Fourth Gospel* (Cambridge: The University Press, 1953), pp. 388–389, 319.

[8]Cf. Hans Urs von Balthasar, *A Theology of History* (New York: Sheed & Ward, 1963), p. 31: "Essentially, [Jesus' hour] is the hour that is *coming*, which, in its coming, is always *there* and therefore determines everything that happens before it and leads up to it, but still has this determinative character as something that is to come, something that cannot be summoned. Not even by knowledge (Mk 13,32), for that too would be an anticipation, disturbing the sheer, naked, unqualified acceptance of what comes from the Father."

[9]An interesting parallel is furnished by Luke's account of the Transfiguration, where Moses and Elijah speak "of his departure (*exodos*), which he was about to (*ēmellen*) accomplish in Jerusalem" (Luke 9,31). Here too the journey to Jerusalem is related both to the Exodus and to the will of God. This helps us understand that Jesus' pilgrimage to the Holy City is far more than a simple road to death: in it is hidden a divine act of liberation. Cf. André Feuillet, "L''Exode' de Jésus et le déroulement du mystère rédempteur d'après S. Luc et S. Jean," *Revue Thomiste* 77 (1977), pp. 181–187.

[10]Feuillet, pp. 193–194, and Dodd, p. 375, mention that the verb "to lift up" is found in the fourth Servant Song in Isa 52–53, where it is used to express the future glorification of the Servant after his ignominious death: "he will be raised and lifted up and highly exalted" (Isa 52,13). Now it is striking to note that in John's gospel, the lifting up of Jesus is always mentioned in connection with the figure of the Son of Man (3,14; 8,28; 12,34). Elsewhere (PGod 181) I have interpreted the vision of the Son of Man in Daniel 7 as the prolongation of the fourth Servant Song seen, so to speak, through God's eyes. This parallel is an indication that the unity emphasized so strongly by John between the death (lifting up on the cross) and the glorification or exaltation (going up to heaven) of Jesus is not simply a brilliant idea of the evangelist. Could not Jesus himself, the Exegete of the Father (John 1,18), have seen this identity between the Servant of Second Isaiah and Daniel's Son of Man as a key for the understanding of his own mission?

[11]The Greek word means only "a morsel, a bit of food," not necessarily a piece of bread. And yet it is not impossible that we have here an allusion to the Eucharist (cf. 13,18).

[12]See Aelred Lacomara, "Deuteronomy and the Farewell Discourse (Jn 13:31—16:33)," *Catholic Biblical Quarterly*, Vol. 36 (1974), pp. 65–84. Cf. also Yves Simoens, *La gloire d'aimer. Structures stylistiques et inter-*

prétatives dans le Discours de la Cène (Jn 13–17) (Rome: Biblical Institute Press, 1981), pp. 202–227; Feuillet, pp. 195–196; Glasson, pp. 74–78.

[13]Lacomara, p. 84.

[14]See De la Potterie, pp. 445–453.

[15]Cf. John Paul II, Encyclical Letter *Dominum et Vivificantem* on the Holy Spirit in the life of the Church and the world (18 May 1986), n. 61.

[16]Godfrey C. Nicholson, *Death as Departure: The Johannine Descent-Ascent Schema* (SBC Dissertation Series, 63), (Chico, CA: Scholars' Press, 1983), p. 165.

[17]The "I am" is a divine title (cf. Ex 3,14). By adopting it, Jesus proclaims that he is of divine status, truly God's only Son, and therefore King in a manner far beyond all human authorities (cf. Ps 95,3; Dan 2,47). See Brown, Appendix IV, pp. 533–538.

[18]The prologue of the fourth gospel already gives us an anticipation of these two dimensions of the way of Jesus, rooting them in the very being of the Son. The Word is "the Only-Begotten [coming] from the Father" (*monogenous para Patros*, 1,14) and also "the Only-Begotten who is [turned] toward the Father's bosom" (*monogenēs ho ōn eis ton kolpon tou Patros*, 1,18; cf. 1,1b). Jesus' career on earth is thus a transcription in human history of his eternal identity. Once more, God has only one thing to reveal to us, and that reality is himself.

"Followers of the Way"

(Acts 9,2)

FIVE

I Am Going before You ...

Given their place at the end of the gospels, it would be easy to consider the accounts of Jesus' resurrection and ascension as the end-point of his way. With the resurrection, we might think, the journey is over, the story is finished; we have now reached the "happy ending" that justifies all that went before it. This view is comprehensible, but insufficient. Certainly, the Good News of the resurrection ratifies Jesus' identity as God's beloved. In the light of that great Day, the disciples can finally begin to grasp the true meaning of past events which up till then had been enigmatic, "veiled" from their sight (e.g. Mark 8,14–21; 9,10.32; John 2,22; 12,16), above all the need for their Master to give his life to the end (Luke 24,7.26). In this respect, the resurrection is a new starting-point in reverse: it motivates a backward glance and leads to a reinterpretation of the past, making the unity of God's plan emerge more clearly. At the same time, far from being a static and self-contained ending, the resurrection represents a new beginning for Jesus' pilgrimage with his disciples "to the ends of the earth" (Acts 1,8). More than ever, the Risen Lord is a pilgrim, still more, the mere encounter with him impels others to set out on the road. Constantly in motion, henceforth he is totally the Way (John 14,6)—the way to the Father and the way to human beings.

A Reality more real than our own

Each of the gospel accounts of the resurrection shows, in its own way, this setting out on a journey, the "passover" from an immobility turned toward a past that is over and done with to a brand-new dynamism. The first announcement of the Good News of the resurrection starts at the tomb where Jesus had been laid to rest. Seemingly impelled by an irresistible force, women who had loved Jesus head toward this place of "memorial," where human beings attempt, by constructions of stone, to counteract the effects of death and to hold on to a happy past, to a loved one who is no longer among them. Whether they come to honor his memory by embalming the corpse (Mark, Luke) or simply to contemplate (Matthew), their desire to keep alive a relationship is, humanly speaking, as understandable and praiseworthy as it is ultimately futile.

Things do not follow their preordained course, however. The women find that the tomb is open and the body gone. Walls built by human beings, and heavy stones, cannot hold back a Life that is stronger than death. To remove any ambiguity, there is the presence of messengers from heaven (reduced to vestiges in John's gospel) who proclaim the Good News: "He is risen; he is not here!" In fact, the sight of the empty tomb is not enough (John 20,3–10; Luke 24,12); a positive encounter with the world beyond death is necessary to provoke a conversion.

More than anywhere else in the gospels (with the possible exception of the stories of Jesus' birth in Matthew and Luke) the accounts of the resurrection are impervious to any facile harmonization. Agreement is not to be found on the literal level of the text, of the "facts" recounted. We are confronted here by a Reality more real than our own, refracted through minds that are insufficiently awake to grasp it adequately. With respect to the life of the resurrection we are barely awake, or possibly still asleep. This Reality attempts to penetrate our understanding like the first sounds of a brand-new day penetrate the dreams of a sleeper. The essential is there, but this Life more powerful than death can never be reduced to the limits of our world here below. The best way to proceed, then, is to enter into the perspective of each gospel, to follow its course and to listen to its call for a reversal of our outlook and a widening of our horizon.

In all the diversity of the different accounts there is, however, one constant: the encounter with the reality of the resurrection sets people on the road. Ordinary women and men all at once become "apostles," people sent out. In Matthew's and Mark's version, the women are told to go to the disciples to transmit a message (Matt 28,7.10; Mark 16,7). John's account shows the same instructions given to Mary of Magdala (John 20,17; cf. Mark 16,10). Luke knows of no such order, but the women (Luke 24,9; cf. John 20,2), as well as the disciples on the road to Emmaus (Luke 24,33–35; cf. Mark 16,13), head spontaneously toward the apostles to recount their experience. The first movement is thus one of being sent toward the community of believers. The Risen Lord's first act is to rebuild a fellowship around the Twelve.

This first encounter with the reality of the resurrection is not, however, sufficient in itself. Luke tells us that, to the apostles, the women's tale "seemed ridiculous, and they did not believe them" (24,11). The theme of doubt, incidentally, is an integral part of the stories of the resurrection, perhaps as a way of reminding us that we are not dealing here with an automatic—and ultimately magical—transformation. It is perhaps not surprising that there is a refusal to believe when the message comes indirectly, through the words of others (Luke 24,11.22–24; Mark 16,11; John 20,25). But even a direct encounter is not always fully convincing (Matt 28,17; John 21,4.12), at least at first (Luke 24,16.37.41; John 20,14). John follows one of his customary procedures by personalizing the theme of doubt in the figure of Thomas (20,24–29), and this enables Jesus to praise all those who believe without having seen.

In general, doubt, the inability to be transformed by the Good News of the resurrection, is a minor theme in the gospel accounts, subordinated to the theme of faith which stimulates a kind of new beginning, a setting out on the road. In Mark's gospel, however, the theme of doubt persists in all its radicalness, for the oldest version of the gospel we can reconstruct concludes with these words: "And they said nothing to anyone, for they were afraid . . ." (Mark 16,8). Fear and the non-transmission of the message as the conclusion of the gospel: this seemed so unacceptable that quickly attempts were made to remedy the situation. On the one hand, it has often been conjectured that an original ending was lost or suppressed. Moreover, early on other endings were composed and admitted into the canon, even if stylistic criteria demonstrate rather conclusively that they come from another pen than that of the evangelist Mark.

Must we therefore resign ourselves to the fact that the text of Mark's gospel has been irretrievably corrupted, or can we attribute a meaning to the version that ends with 16,8? Yes, if we remember that this gospel as a whole was written in the light of the resurrection of Jesus, which gives us the certainty that he is the Messiah, the Son of God (1,1). At the heart of this book (9,2–8), we find the episode of the transfiguration of Jesus, a clear portrait of his glorified condition. And at the very end we encounter a young man garbed in white, a figure of the evangelist (16,5; cf. 14,51), who proclaims, "He is risen . . . he is going before you to Galilee; there you will see him" (16,6–7). Now Galilee, the place where Matthew and Mark situate the definitive encounter with the Risen Lord, is the opposite extreme from the center of the nation where Jesus' condemnation and death took place. "Galilee of the nations" (Matt 4,15) is a place where Gentiles and Jews live side by side, a place symbolizing inclusion, not exclusion. From the viewpoint of spiritual geography, Galilee thus represents the periphery, "the ends of the earth," the wide world bequeathed as missionary territory to the Christian community. Thus for Mark, could not the words of the young man in white be seen as an invitation to the community of disciples to set out towards the horizon in the wake of the risen Christ? In this perspective the appearances of the Risen Lord would be secondary; the important thing is the encounter which each of us will have as we set out in faith, and the definitive encounter that will mark the end of time.

If this is in fact Mark's intention (and, given the state of the text, this is impossible to determine), it is interesting that Matthew provides a confirmation, in another manner, of this priority accorded to our present and future encounter with the risen Christ with respect to the Easter appearances in Palestine. The first gospel ends in an encounter with Christ on a mountain in Galilee (28,16–20), but here we have something far different than the more intimate meetings described by Luke and John. In Matt 28, the Risen Lord is not a man among men who shows his wounds, eats or prepares a meal; he is the formidable Pantocrator of a Byzantine mosaic, the Lord on whom unlimited authority is bestowed in space ("in heaven and on earth . . . all nations") and time ("always, until the end of the age"). He is Emmanuel, God-with-us for all time. This is a synthetic, meta-historical vision, in which resurrection and final coming coincide, within which the entire history of the Christian Church is played out, somewhat like in a basilica of the East in which all the liturgical activity takes place under the gaze of the Pantocrator depicted on the dome. It is, at the same time, an extremely dynamic vision: the Lord sends his disciples throughout the world ("Go therefore . . . ") and promises to accompany them on all their pilgrimages.

Luke and John tell of a similar sending out, but in a different way. The Risen Lord meets the community of disciples at Jerusalem, in the upper room, probably around a table (cf. Mark 16,14), the evening of the day of his resurrection. In John (20,19–23), we see a clear transition from the group of disciples locked up in fear (v. 19) to the peace (vv. 19,21) and joy (v. 20) that the risen Christ brings into their closed world. As always, his presence is a call to set out on the road, and here the way of the disciples is strictly parallel to the way of Jesus himself: "As the Father has sent me, so I am sending you" (v. 21b). By the gift of the Holy Spirit, the disciples become a source of forgiveness for the world (vv. 22–23). If the first act of the risen Christ was to re-form the community of disciples which had been scattered by the powers of evil, his second act is to dilate this community to the dimensions of "the whole world" (Mark 16,15) by an invitation to set out, linked to the gift of the Spirit.

The fulfillment of the past

As usual Luke, with his historian's mentality, is the one who distinguishes the different phases most clearly. Chapter 24 of his gospel brings together all the appearances of the risen Christ leading up to the ascension in a single day, a day which is symbolic ("the Day of the Lord") and not chronological (cf. Acts 1,3). Similarly, everything takes place in and around the city of Jerusalem: there is no mention of an encounter in Galilee, and the sending out on mission is postponed to a later date. Instead, everything leads towards the Holy City and the community of the disciples, who are instructed by Christ before he goes up to heaven. His main concern is to help them grasp the unity of

God's plan, to open their minds to an understanding of the Scriptures (vv. 27,45) and especially to the necessity of his death and its link to the resurrection: "Did not the Messiah have to (*dei*) suffer these things and so enter into his glory?" (v. 26; cf. vv. 7,46).

Jesus turns the disciples' eyes to the past ("Remember," v. 6), but not in a vain attempt to keep alive what is dead and gone, to try and nullify the passage of time. On the contrary, now this past is meaningful because it has been *fulfilled* by the passover of Christ (v. 44). Given meaning in this way, it can witness to the continuity of the Father's faithful love; it tells of God's mercy "from age to age" (Luke 1,50). Time is no longer the arena where separation and alienation are inevitably triumphant; for believers it delineates the features of a God of love.

This transformation can be clearly perceived in the story of the disciples of Emmaus, the heart of Luke 24. The two men who leave Jerusalem know the whole story of Jesus' life up to and including the empty tomb (vv. 19–24), but that in itself cannot take away their profound sadness (v. 17). Only the presence of the Risen Lord who reveals the meaning of the events by interpreting the Scriptures (vv. 25–27) and shows himself to them in the breaking of the bread (vv. 30–31) is able to transform this history into *kerygma*, into the proclamation of Good News. All at once their past is shown to have been animated by the hidden presence of the Lord (v. 32). At the same time the future opens before them: the two disciples run towards the community in Jerusalem to tell the news and to share their joy. There they discover that an identical experience now unites them, for "the Lord is risen and has appeared to Simon!" (v. 34).

The last words of the risen Christ recorded by Saint Luke point out the road of the future in the context of the eternal designs of God:

> Thus it is written that Christ would suffer and rise from the dead on the third day, and that in his name a change of heart and the forgiveness of sins would be proclaimed to all nations, beginning from Jerusalem. You are witnesses to this. And see, I am going to send what my Father has promised upon you. So remain in the city until you are clothed with power from on high. (vv. 46–49)

Jerusalem is a terminus, since from the time of the prophets of old it was held that the definitive intervention of the God of Israel would involve a universal gathering in the transformed Holy City (cf. Isa 2,2–3a; Isa 60–62). But it is also a starting-point, the place from which a new world order radiates outward (Isa 2,3b-4). And so, for this new stage, this centrifugal movement, to begin, the disciples must wait in the city until they receive from Christ "what my Father has promised . . . power from on high" (v. 49). And the gospel ends with a view of Jesus rising to the Father in the act of blessing his disciples (vv. 50–51). To bless someone, in the Bible, means to give them an increase of life; in this case, the life Jesus gives is his own, an inexhaustible font of life for those who believe in him. Far from being the sign of an absence, the ascension inaugurates a new kind of presence, along the same lines as the finale of Matthew's gospel. This is clear from the "great joy" that fills the hearts of the disciples, and the unceasing current of praise that rises to heaven from the Temple (v.53). "He blessed them . . . they were in the Temple blessing God." Henceforth a great river of life flows between heaven and earth, an unbreakable communion unites God and the created world.

To the ends of the earth

In spite of this impressive ending, it is clear that Luke's work would be incomplete if it stopped at the end of his gospel. Without a sending out on mission, without the proclamation of God's forgiveness to all nations (cf. Luke 24,47), the way of the Lord is lacking an essential element. The total fulfilment of the prophetic oracles has not yet come about.[1] For this reason, Luke continues his account in a second book, the ACTS OF THE APOSTLES. Here the pilgrimage of the risen Christ is almost imperceptibly transformed into the pilgrimage of the disciples, a transformation made possible by the gift of the Holy Spirit. In the existence of the Christian community animated and sustained by the Spirit, the Risen Lord continues his pilgrimage on earth: the Good News of the Kingdom sets out from Jerusalem, crosses Palestine, Asia Minor and Europe to reach "the ends of the earth" (Acts 1,8b; cf. Isa 49,6) symbolized by Rome, the capital of the pagan world.

The beginning of Acts brings us back to the time before the ascension of Jesus. We see the community of disciples receiving a formation for the new phase that will soon begin. The Risen Lord instructs them for a period of forty days (1,2–3), a biblical number that, since the Exodus, stands for a time of preparation, of transition, as between Egypt and Canaan (Deut 8,2) or between the baptism and the public ministry of Jesus (Mark 1,13). After this preparation, the new stage will begin with a baptism in the Holy Spirit (1,5), a baptism similar to the one that the Lord himself had received (Luke 3,21–22).

When the apostles ask Jesus a question about the time when the Kingdom will be restored to Israel, he gives them this significant reply:

> It is not for you to know the times and dates that the Father has set by his own authority. But you will receive power when the Holy Spirit comes upon you, and you will be my witnesses in Jerusalem, in all of Judea and Samaria, and to the ends of the earth. (1,7–8)

On first hearing, these words are disappointing. They appear to be a refusal to reveal God's plan, reserved to the Father alone. When we look more closely, however, we discover that the essential has been communicated. Although no global, exterior view of God's intention is possible, nevertheless the apostles will discover this intention by living it out, day by day. They will be given all they need when they receive the Holy Spirit, which will make them witnesses to Christ. It is a typically human desire to want to know all the details of an enterprise before committing oneself to it. Human, but in the final analysis illusory, since it would turn us into robots condemned to execute step by step a preconceived plan. God's will or "plan" is not like this: it does not replace or destroy human freedom but liberates it, in other words enables it fully to come into its own.

A second very significant consequence follows from this first one. God's design, the restoration of the Kingdom, is basically for Luke *a way to be followed*. It is a pilgrimage with three stages: first in the city of Jerusalem, then throughout Palestine, and finally to the ends of the earth. Here we have the table of contents of the Acts of the Apostles; the rest of the book will flesh out this framework. It is no accident, then, that for Luke, the most accurate name for the Christian life is "the Way"[2], since it is above all a being-on-the-road under the guidance of the Holy Spirit.

Once his instructions have been given, the risen Christ goes off (*poreuomai*, 1,10) to heaven as the disciples look on. In this way, like Elisha with his master Elijah (2 Kings 2,9–12), they are sure to receive a share in his spirit.[3] They do not have to keep their eyes on the sky while waiting passively for his return; already here on earth a vast field of activity is opening up before them.

The disciples—both men and women—then return to the city and persevere in prayer "with one accord" (1,12–14). The first image we have of them is thus that of a community in prayer, a living icon of communion with God and among human beings. This community has a certain structure which must be maintained. Judas' place must be filled (1,15–26) so that the college of apostles can still have twelve members, a number that evokes the recapitulation of all Israel ("the twelve tribes") in the Kingdom of God.

All the dry wood has now been gathered, but the spark that will light the fire is still missing. It comes on the feast of Pentecost, a Jewish high holy day that commemorates the covenant between God and his people, ratified by the gift of the Torah on Mount Sinai (Ex 19). This year, however, the celebration is not simply a memorial of the past but an authentic fulfillment, a renewal. Along the lines of the oracle of the prophet Jeremiah (Jer 31,31–34), from now on God's Law is written not on tablets of stone (Ex 31,18) but on the hearts of the faithful by the gift of God's own Spirit (Acts 2,3–4; cf. Ezek 36,26–27). There immediately follows a gathering of "all nations"; disparities of background and language are overcome by a miraculous unity, the work of the Spirit (2,5–11). In reality, the bystanders are only Jews from different regions of the known world who reside in Jerusalem, but Luke sees in this fact the definitive fulfillment of ancient prophecies. Likewise Peter, in his discourse to the crowd to explain the event, quotes the oracle of the prophet Joel concerning the Spirit sent out "upon all flesh" (2,17ff; cf. Joel 2,28–32) even though the group is in fact a significantly more limited one than the whole of humanity. This is another example of the surprising logic of the Gospel: on Pentecost Day everything is already fulfilled, but like a tiny seed. The fulfillment in no way excludes further growth.[4] The absolute future enters into human history not as a static conclusion but as a permanent source of fruitfulness, as an invitation to set out on the road.

From then on, Luke constantly points to the presence of the Holy Spirit in the Christian community as the true source of its life and its activity. When the crowd looks at the disciples on Pentecost Day, they see and hear the Spirit (2,33). When people lie to Peter, they lie to the Spirit; they put the Spirit to the test (5,3.9). The Spirit sets apart Paul and Barnabas and sends them out on mission (13,2.4). Later on, the Spirit prevents Paul and Silas "from preaching the Word in Asia" and "from entering Bithynia" (16,6–7). Speaking through Christian prophets, the Spirit warns Paul of the danger lying in wait for him on his journey up to Jerusalem (20,23; 21,4.11). And finally, the Spirit builds up the Christian community by naming overseers (*episkopoi*) or shepherds (20,28). The believers do not act in their own name, nor do they merely follow their own inclinations. They have the impression that they are obeying an impulse that comes from somewhere beyond them, that they are being led by Another. That is the reason why the apostles can write to the faithful of Antioch these incredible-sounding words: "It seemed good to the Holy Spirit and to us . . ." (15,28; cf. 5,32).

If the Christian community is deeply conscious that its life is rooted in the Holy Spirit who is also "the Spirit of Jesus" (16,7), that is because it continues in a mysterious manner Jesus' own presence on earth. This was clearly understood by a man named Saul of Tarsus, a Pharisee bitterly hostile to what was in his eyes a new heretical Jewish sect. An experience he had one day on the road to Damascus transformed his own life and the history of the world. Luke tells the story three different times, a clear indication of how important it was for him:

> He was nearing Damascus on his journey, when suddenly a light from heaven enveloped him, and falling to the ground he heard a voice say to him, "Saul, Saul, why are you persecuting me?" "Who are you, Lord?" he asked. "I am Jesus, whom you are persecuting," came the reply. (9,3–5; cf. 22,6–8; 26,13–15)

"I am Jesus, whom you are persecuting." In the life of believers the Risen Lord is still suffering; in them Jesus continues his pilgrimage to the ends of the earth. The way of Christ becomes

126

the way of Christians; he is the Road on which they travel. And so, we can understand why, for Luke, to become a part of the Christian community is "to be added to the Lord" (11,24; 5,14).

The author of Acts emphasizes the similarities between the life of Christians and the life of their Master. Like him, the apostles teach and heal the sick. Jesus both spoke to the crowds in general and "explained everything in private to his own disciples" (Mark 4, 34), and the apostles' teaching likewise has two aspects to it: a proclamation of the essential elements of the Good News—the life, death and especially the resurrection of Jesus as fulfillment of the Scriptures—meant for those outside the community, and a more detailed explanation for those who are already part of the group (2,42; 5,42; 15,32.35). Luke reports this teaching in long discourses which occupy a large part of his book.

Then there are the acts of healing. Immediately after the events of Pentecost, we see Peter and John in the Temple curing a lame man "in the name of Jesus Christ the Nazarene" (3,1–10). The man, formerly rooted to the spot, is henceforth able to walk, and even to run, along the road. Other acts of healing performed by Peter (9,32–35) and by Philip (8,7) are mentioned, and even the story of a woman brought back to life (9,36–42). Paul, in his turn, heals (14,8–10; 19,11–12), casts out a doubtful spirit (16,18), and raises someone from death (20,7–12). But all this is only possible because of the presence of Jesus (9,34; 16,18), or God (4,30), at work in those who have been sent out.

As during the earthly ministry of Jesus, the presence of God's Newness in words and deeds provokes a spontaneous movement toward it. This is what happens because of the healings:

By the hands of the apostles many signs and wonders were accomplished among the people . . . to such an extent that sick people were brought into the streets and laid on beds and mats so that when Peter came by his shadow might fall on one of them. Crowds even came from the towns around Jerusalem, bringing the sick and those possessed by unclean spirits, and all were cured. (5,12.15–16)

A similar result follows from the apostles' preaching. After Peter's speech on Pentecost Day, Luke tells us that "about three thousand souls were added to their number that day" (2,41b).

And throughout the book of Acts he continually mentions the growth of the community (2,47; 4,4; 5,14; 11,21 etc.).

The other side of this prodigious expansion, a sign of the presence of God's Spirit, quickly makes itself felt: the opposition which comes especially from the leaders of the people. Prisons occupy an important place in the story of the life of the early Christians, and this will be true throughout the centuries whenever the Church witnesses authentically to the Gospel message. By these accounts of persecution Luke counterbalances the "triumphal" aspect of the way of the Church. It may well have been true that the first Christians "were held in esteem by all the people" (2,47; cf. 4,33b; 5,13); it is no less true that beginning on the day after Pentecost they encountered hostility. Immediately following the first cure performed by Peter and John, they were arrested and had to appear before the Sanhedrin (ch. 4). And that is only the first of a long series of hardships that believers will have to endure: stays in prison (5,18; 8,3; 12,4; 16,23; 21,34), appearances in court (5,27; 6,12; 17,6; 18,12; 22,30; 24,1; 25,6.23), violence (5,40; 16,22; 18,17; 19,23ff; 21,30f; 23,10), persecutions (8,1; 13,50) and even an execution (7,55–60). In this way the disciples follow to the letter the way of their Master, the way of the cross.

And yet, just as for their Master, the failure is only apparent. Human malice never has the last word. Paradoxically, the persecutions contribute to the success of the Gospel. Following the death of Stephen, for example, a persecution breaks out and leads to the scattering of believers "throughout the regions of Judea and Samaria" (8,1). And the account continues: "Those who had been forced to flee went from place to place proclaiming the Word" (8,4). The second phase of the expansion of the Church (cf. 1,8) then begins. Persecuted, scattered, the young Church becomes a missionary body.

Similarly, Luke links the theme of persecution to the first time the Good News is proclaimed to non-Jews. This happens in Antioch, and it is the work of "those who had been scattered by the troubles that occurred around Stephen" (11,19a). A while later, Paul and his companions are chased from town to town by the jealous opposition of some of his countrymen (13,50; 14,5–6.20; 17,5.10.14 etc.) and in this way the evangelization of the Mediterranean world goes forward. In his ministry, Paul turns to the Gentiles whenever the Jews in the towns he visits refuse his message (13,46; 18,6). The Acts of the Apostles even concludes with this statement of his teacher Paul which is so important for Luke: "It is to the Gentiles that this salvation of God has been sent; at least they will listen to it" (28,28). Israel's misstep has brought salvation to the Gentiles (Rom 11,11), thus witnessing to the unfathomable wisdom and the universal mercy of God (Rom 11,30–36).

Sending and gathering

The portrait of the first Christians drawn in the Acts of the Apostles has two main aspects. Together they form the diastole and systole of the life of the Church, the beating of its heart.[5]

The first aspect is represented above all by the Church of Jerusalem gathered around the Twelve. We have already noticed how, in his account of Pentecost, Luke sees the fulfillment of all the prophecies regarding a universal gathering of the nations in the Holy City, even though "in reality" it seems to have been a more limited event. And yet, on another level, Luke is right to attribute an eschatological significance to the appearance of the Christian Church as a consequence of the resurrection of Jesus. The "last days" have become a reality in the existence of a community that makes present in human history God's own life, a communion with no boundaries. It is this above all that Luke wants us to grasp in his well-known descriptions of the life of the early Christians:

> They were faithful to the apostles' teaching, to the common life, to the breaking of bread and to the prayers. Everyone was filled with awe; many signs and wonders were done by the apostles. All the believers were together and shared everything in common. They would sell their property and possessions and share the proceeds among all, according to the needs of each. Every day they would meet together in the Temple united in mind and heart, going to one another's homes for the breaking of bread, sharing their food in gladness and simplicity of heart, praising God and enjoying the esteem of all the people. (2,42–47a; cf. 4,32–35; 5,12–16).

Prayer and sharing, two expressions of communion. We might be inclined to convict the author of these lines of romanticism, of an inability to see things as they are. And yet elsewhere, Luke depicts with absolutely no hesitation the sins and divisions that mar the life of the community from the very beginning (e.g. 5,1ff; 6,1; 15,39). The true significance of these descriptions has nothing to do with human idealism or naivete. They are there to help us realize that in the existence of the Christian community, the covenant between God and creation has been fully ratified. Henceforth, on this earth, there exists the real possibility of a communion with no barriers, of a universal reconciliation. This communion is already present in microcosm; human hatred and violence can no longer prevent its becoming a reality (cf. Matt 16,18; John 16,33).

Luke thus identifies the eschatological aspect of the Church with the Jerusalem community, and more generally with the theme of *gathering*. We know that the Christians of Jerusalem were the first ones to receive the eschatological title "the saints" (e.g. Acts 9,13; 1 Cor 16,1; cf. Dan 7,18), a title which later on was employed in all the Christian communities.[6] In the expression used only by Luke, "the twelve apostles" (cf. Acts 1,26), the title "the Twelve" indicates more particularly this dimension of gathering since it is an allusion to the ingathering of all the tribes of Israel. Each time the community comes together in one place, then, especially for common prayer, it prefigures this definitive gathering of all humanity in the Kingdom of God. It already tastes something of heaven's joy on earth, and in this way becomes, consciously or not, a magnet that attracts others.[7]

The Church gathered together in unity, first-fruits of the Kingdom: that is still only one side of its identity. The Acts show us even more clearly the other principal aspect of the Christian life, the pilgrimage on the road. For Luke, the Twelve are also *apostles*, people sent out to bring the message of salvation to the very ends of the earth. It cannot be emphasized too strongly that the entry of the *eschaton*, the absolute future, in the midst of our history is in no way an automatic ending, the cessation of all human activity in the face of the overwhelming power of God. On the contrary, this entry is a dynamic principle of expansion, a sending out towards others.

Luke is eager to show this other dimension of the Christian life, existence on the roads. Journeying is an integral part of an apostle's identity. Speaking of Peter, he uses this surprising expression, hard to translate: "Peter, who went everywhere, from place to place (*dierchomenon dia pantōn*) ..." (9,32). Paul is even more a traveller who goes (*dieporeunto*) from town to town (16,4; 20,23) to announce the Good News everywhere, but also to strengthen the Churches (15,41) by his visits (15,36). Visits between Christians thus become, early on, one of the most important means of creating communion through mutual support. The young Church takes on more and more the aspect of a network of communion that gradually covers the whole inhabited world with its links.

The framework of the Acts of the Apostles is formed essentially by this expansion of the Christian community. Impelled by the presence of the Holy Spirit who often acts through seemingly unfavorable events, the "followers of the Way" (9,2) leave Jerusalem, cross Judea and Samaria, travel to Asia Minor and to Europe until at last they arrive in Rome, capital of the Empire and thus the center of the known world. In the first part of the book, Peter is the standard-bearer of this expansion, but soon his place is taken by Paul, the former Pharisee and adversary of the Church transformed into a tireless missionary especially to the pagans (9,15; 22,21; 26,17).

The difficulties of the journey and the obstacles to be overcome are not only material and geographical, although in fact the hardships of travel, especially on the sea, are often recounted at length (e.g. ch. 27; cf. 2 Cor 11,25f). The central question of the book, however, concerns the widening of the offer of salvation to non-Jews without requiring them to accept all the requirements of the Torah and to become Jews. For the first Christians, this was not at all obvious, since they had no sense of having started a new religion. One of the principal concerns of the author of Acts is to demonstrate how, little by little, God enlightened the disciples to resolve this question.

The Acts of the Apostles show us this widening of the Christian community, step by step, by describing the increasing diversity of its members. The apostles are all Jews from Palestine and, even though in the experience of Pentecost a certain universality is anticipated by all the languages and countries mentioned, Luke states quite clearly that the crowd is in fact made up of Jews residing in Jerusalem (2,5.11). Later on we hear talk of Hebrews and Hellenists (6,1), so we know that the community came to include Aramaic-speaking Jews born in Palestine as well as those whose language and culture was Greek. The next stage follows the death of Stephen, when Philip announces the Good News to the Samaritans, "cousins" of the Jews (8,4–8). After this Luke places the account of the baptism of an Ethiopian eunuch (8,26–40). This story comes at the appropriate place because we are incapable of determining for sure whether this royal functionary is a Jewish convert or not; in any case he is an individual very different in background from the believers we have met up to now, a sign of the growing diversity in the community.[8]

Still, the great turning-point of the book is yet to come: the opening of the community to include pagans. This story is told in chapter 10. Following a vision and clear proofs of the presence of the Holy Spirit, Peter baptizes Cornelius, a Roman centurion, as well as his relatives and friends. He has finally understood that "God makes no distinctions among persons, but people of any nation who are God-fearing and do what is right are pleasing to him" (10,34–35). Peter then has to justify his conduct and calm the fears of the Jerusalem community (11,1–18), but the essential step has been taken: "Greeks" (11,20) can join the group of believers without being required to be circumcised beforehand. We have now truly entered the new age predicted by the prophets, the time when salvation is available to all the nations. The controversy will spring up anew as a result of a difference of opinion in Antioch, and "the apostles and the elders" will study the question in greater depth (ch. 15). They will come to the same conclusion, however, and will write a letter to the Christians of Antioch to share with them what "seemed good to the Holy Spirit and to us" (15,28). This should not be seen as an attempt to force God's hand but rather to discern what God is undertaking in the world through the events of human history (cf. 10,47; 11,17; 15,8).

Now that the road to the Gentiles has been opened, the center of interest of the book shifts from Peter and the Jerusalem Church to Paul and his missionary journeys in Asia Minor and Europe. As soon as Paul arrives in a city, he goes to the synagogue to proclaim the Gospel, but when the Jews refuse to listen he turns to the Gentiles. In this way both the priority due to the chosen people and the new post-Pentecost universality are expressed. At the end of his missions, "Paul decided to cross Macedonia and Achaia and to journey to Jerusalem" (19,21).

This gives Luke the opportunity to show once again the parallel between the way of Christ and the way of the Christian. Like that of his Lord, Paul's journey to the Holy City is shown to be a road of suffering and death:

> And now look, bound by the Spirit I am going up to Jerusalem, where I do not know what will happen to me, except that, from town to town, the Holy Spirit has been warning me that chains and troubles are lying in wait for me. (20,22–23)

There is even a prophecy of his fate that sounds like one of the prophecies of the passion of Jesus (21,11; cf. Luke 18,32). For his part Paul is prepared: "I am ready not only to be imprisoned, but even to die in Jerusalem for the name of the Lord Jesus" (21,13).

Paul does not die in Jerusalem, but his presence leads to rioting and to his arrest by the Romans. Several attempts to prove his innocence follow, before the Sanhedrin (23,1–10), before Felix the governor (ch. 24), before King Agrippa (ch. 26). In this way, according to the prophetic words of Jesus, Paul is able to bear witness to the Name of Jesus "before kings and governors" (Luke 21,12–13). He finally appeals to the emperor, and is brought in chains to the city of Rome. The book concludes with his stay in that city; he is seen "proclaiming the Kingdom of God and teaching all about the Lord Jesus Christ with full confidence and with no hindrance" (28,31). Believers will continue to walk along the way of the Lord: from Rome, the center of the "inhabited world," new missionary journeys will set out. But for the author of Acts, the essential has already been recounted. The way of the Risen Lord, involving "many hardships" (14,22) but always sustained by the power of the Holy Spirit (1,8a), has reached the ends of the earth (1,8b). The execution of a condemned man in an obscure and remote province of the Roman empire has liberated a power of communion that "has turned the whole world upside down" (cf. 17,6).

Questions for Reflection

1. The proclamation of Jesus' resurrection and the encounters with the Risen Lord are not so much an end as a beginning. In this respect, what is the significance of Mark 16,1–8? Is it possible that Mark's gospel could have ended in this way? Why or why not?

2. In the accounts of the resurrection we can distinguish two movements: a centripetal movement, toward the community of believers, and a centrifugal movement, a movement outward. Give examples of each of these movements. What is the significance of each for the Christian pilgrimage? Can something similar be detected in the life of the first Christians described in the Acts of the Apostles?

3. Why did Luke write a second book, the Acts of the Apostles, as a complement to his gospel? Should the other gospel writers have done the same thing?

4. In the book of Acts, Christianity is referred to as "the Way" (Acts 9,2; 18,26; 19,9.23 etc.). What is the importance of this term? How can the portrait of the early Church given in this book help us to understand and live out our faith today?

Notes

[1]See Jacques Dupont, "La portée christologique de l'évangélisation des nations," *Nouvelles études sur les Actes des Apôtres* (Paris: Cerf, 1984) pp. 37–57.

[2]Cf. p. 14.

[3]*Une lecture des Actes des Apôtres*, Cahiers evangile, 21 (Paris: Cerf, 1977), p. 19.

[4]Cf. the refrain found throughout the book of Acts: "the Word of the Lord (God) grew" (6,7; 12,24; 19,20).

[5]Here I have drawn inspiration from the remarks of the Orthodox theologian John D. Zizioulas on "The Two Approaches, 'Historical' and 'Eschatological', to Apostolic Continuity" in his article "Apostolic Continuity and Succession," chapter 5 of his book *Being as Communion: Studies in Personhood and the Church* (Crestwood, NY: St. Vladimir's Seminary Press, 1985), pp. 172ff.

[6]Cf. NJB, note *g* on Acts 9,13, p. 1813.

[7]The Eastern Churches make us particularly attentive to this eschatological dimension of the Church, first-fruits of the Kingdom already present on this earth, especially during the celebration of the holy liturgy. This also explains the importance given to the resurrection of Christ in Orthodox spirituality, a valuable corrective to the more historical, cross-centered piety of Western Christians. Cf. Zizioulas, pp. 171, 181–182.

[8]Cf. Ernst Haenchen, *Die Apostelgeschichte* (Göttingen: Vandenhoeck & Ruprecht, 1956), pp. 271–272.

SIX

Paul,
Seized by Christ

Our discovery that the Christian faith is a way, a pilgrimage undertaken by the risen Christ at the heart of human history, finds a confirmation in the simple fact that the last half of the New Testament is composed essentially of letters written to Christian communities in the process of formation. Whereas the first books of the New Testament recount the life of a man in whom the way of the Lord becomes manifest, in the following writings this way takes the form of a network of communion that links the cities of the Mediterranean world. Even if, for didactic purposes, a certain systematization sometimes makes itself felt, the apostolic letters are motivated above all by the concerns of the present, by existential questions. Rather than to transmit a code of behavior (a "law") or to speculate on the mysteries of God, their main purpose is to create and to maintain bonds of faith, hope and love between men and women whose lives have been transformed by the coming of Christ. This purpose must be kept in mind as we investigate the content of these letters.

Most of the epistles of the New Testament are attributed to Saint Paul. They are a reflection of the tireless efforts of this apostle of the last hour (cf. 1 Cor 15,8) to bring the Good News of Jesus Christ to the wide world of the non-Jews, "to Greeks

as well as to barbarians, to the educated as well as to the igno-
rant" (Rom 1,14). After he has spent time in a city, Paul feels
responsible for the life of the community he has set up there.
"Concern for all the churches" (2 Cor 11,28) is his daily obses-
sion, and exchanging letters is one way of compensating for the
inability to be there in person. The fact that these letters were
later collected in the canon of the Christian Scriptures proves
that their significance is far greater than the particular situation
of the communities to which they were addressed, that they
have a permanent importance for believers. Over and above all
the evolutions of society and culture, today we are on the same
road, we participate in the same communion that brought together women and men in the cities of the Mediterranean world
two thousand years ago.

Born into a new Life

Chronologically speaking, the first writings of the New Testament are the two letters written by Paul to the THESSALONIANS
close to the year 51, shortly after his apostolic activity in that city
(cf. Acts 17,1–10).[1] They are among the most personal, the least
systematic of Paul's letters. Their great interest resides in the
fact that they explain the Christian way in an almost "naive"
fashion. The faith has not yet found its technical vocabulary, its
clearly defined doctrines. The essential aspects of the Christian
reality can thus be discovered, so to speak, "in the raw"; seeds
are present that will be developped by Paul and by others for
years and centuries to come.

In writing to the faithful of Thessalonica, Paul feels the need
to remind them at length about the origins of their faith. As in
the Hebrew Scriptures and in the gospels, historical events as
such are bearers of meaning. What will later be called Christianity is neither a philosophy, a theory or an ideology, but the
transmission of a Life. It is a way of life, a spiritual journey (1
Thess 2,12; 4,1.12 *peripatein*).

This Life was transmitted to the Thessalonians by Paul. The
apostle came to them to proclaim "the Good News of God" (1
Thess 1,5; 2,1–12). This Good News was not merely a matter of
words, of ideas about God: for Paul it was at the same time the
gift of his own life (1 Thess 2,8). And along with the message,

the power of the Holy Spirit was communicated to the hearers (1 Thess 1,5). They understood then that it was not merely human words but God's own creative Word at work within them (1 Thess 2,13), that God had chosen them and offered them his love (1 Thess 1,4; 2 Thess 2,13). In welcoming this Word (1 Thess 1,6), the Thessalonians began to lead a life of faith, love and hope (1 Thess 1,3). This was the work in them of God who is faithful, and so Paul is sure that God will carry it to completion (2 Thess 1,11; 1 Thess 5,24).

Since it is a question of the birth of a new life in them, Paul can compare himself to a father (1 Thess 2,11; cf. 1 Cor 4,15), and even to a mother (1 Thess 2,7; cf. 2 Cor 6,13; 12,14; Gal 4,19). And just as in a relationship between biological parents and children, *imitation* has an important role to play. Over and above all intellectual explanations, one enters into a life by looking at the way others live and by acting in consequence. Paul consciously offers himself to the new believers as a model to be imitated (2 Thess 3,7.9), and he writes these astonishing words: "And you became imitators of us, and of the Lord" (1 Thess 1,6; cf. 1 Cor 11,1). What the Thessalonians follow in Paul is not some particular form of human behavior but the way of Christ, and especially the paschal mystery, God's joy in the midst of human difficulties.[2]

In the same way, the Christians of Thessalonica imitate "the Churches of God in Christ Jesus that are in Judea" (1 Thess 2,14), and in their turn they become a model for others (1 Thess 1,7). Mutual emulation becomes a kind of rule of life for believers. Of course there are traditions handed down by Paul that must be kept (2 Thess 2,15); the apostle sometimes gives instructions that come from the Lord Jesus himself (1 Thess 4,1–2). Nevertheless, it is the presence of the Spirit of the risen Christ in the life of the community, and not an exterior code of laws, that represents the essential criterion for judging a believer's life (cf 1 Thess 4,8–9). By deepening their communion with the Lord and among themselves, Christians discover and live out their own identity to an ever greater extent.

In addition to imitation and mutual edification, Paul mentions other expressions of this communion. First and foremost there is *prayer*. The apostle constantly remembers his flock in his prayers, offering for them a continual act of thanksgiving (1 Thess 1,2; 2,13; 3,9; 2 Thess 1,3; 2,13). He asks in turn for their prayers for his ministry (1 Thess 5,25; 2 Thess 3,1). Next there is mutual *encouragement* or comforting, what we might call the human face of the Church. By sharing news, by visiting one another, by seeing the faces of dear friends (cf. 1 Thess 2,17), ties of affection among believers grow ever deeper. The creation and consolidation of such ties are in no way a secondary or optional aspect of the life of the Church but rather an expression of its essence. If a large part of Paul's letters deal with questions of human relationships, that is because he realizes that, beyond specific cases, he is confronted with the most important dimension of his mission—the building up of a brotherly and sisterly communion. It is a matter of making the love of God a concrete reality in a social fabric.

Thus the apostle, filled with an "intense longing" to see the Thessalonians once again and prevented from carrying out his intention, finally sends his co-worker Timothy to them (1 Thess 2,17ff). Timothy offers strength and encouragement to the faithful in the midst of their trials, and the good news about them that he brings back to Paul is likewise a comfort to the apostle in the midst of his own difficulties. Being a believer in this world is never without its troubles and suffering (1 Thess 2,14; 3,4; 2 Thess 1,4–5); it is a struggle (1 Thess 5,8), and that is why it is essential to encourage and to build one another up in order to persevere (1 Thess 5,11). Caring for one another in this way is one of the means by which God comforts and strengthens believers (2 Thess 2,16–17; cf. 2 Cor 1,3–7).

The new Life transmitted by Paul in his ministry of evangelization is thus basically a life in *community*. Though it is first of all a gift from God, this Life must nonetheless lead those who accept it to specific choices, to a way or style of life. Ordinarily, then, at the end of his letters Paul gives advice to suggest to the faithful how they should behave. After having spoken of the gift they have received, he exhorts them to keep leading lives (literally "to walk, *peripatein*") consistent with that gift. "[We urge you] to walk in a way worthy of God who has called you to his Kingdom and his glory . . . you have learned from us how you must walk so as to please God, and that is how you are walking; go even further . . . in such a way that those outside respect you . . ." (1 Thess 2,12; 4,1.12). Christians must become more and more what they are in the depths of their being; the life they live must correspond ever more closely to their true identity, the result of a gift.

Should we be surprised, then, that the instructions that Paul gives deal above all with life together? The apostle exhorts the Thessalonians to live with each other in harmony and love (1 Thess 5,13b-15), showing particular concern for the leaders of the community (1 Thess 5,12–13a) and seeing that each member fills the role allotted to him or her (2 Thess 3,6–15). The faithful should live in joy and in prayer (1 Thess 5,16–18), remaining alert and clear-minded (1 Thess 5,6), quick to discern and to foster the gifts with which the Spirit has graced them (1 Thess 5,19–21). The presence of the Spirit in their midst is a source of holiness, a call to let unruly passions be transfigured into the serene force of love (1 Thess 4,3–12).

Since Christian faith is fundamentally a gift, it could be seen as a static reality, given once and for all and admitting no evolution. To avoid this pitfall, it is important to remember that this gift is that of a Life, of a Way. Faith is a dynamic principle of unlimited fruitfulness. Christians are men and women on pilgrimage, walking in the footsteps of their Master; constant growth is the law of their existence. Paul is extremely attentive to this dimension of growth, of progress in faith, and he points to its source: the Word of God permanently at work in the life of believers (1 Thess 2,13), a Word that must "run forward" (2 Thess 3,1). He urges them to move ahead on the road: "go even further ... we encourage you, brothers and sisters, to go still further" (1 Thess 4,1b.10b). He writes to the Thessalonians that "your faith is growing and the love you all have for each other is increasing" (2 Thess 1,3b). And he prays: "may the Lord lead your hearts into the love of God and the perseverance of Christ ... may the Lord make you increase and overflow in love for one another and for all" (2 Thess 3,5; 1 Thess 3,12). In the Christian life, progress is essentially a growth in love, its constant deepening and widening.

In Paul's mind, does this progress ever come to an end? Can we determine the ultimate horizon of his vision? Here we have, formulated in other terms, the question of Christian eschatology, an extremely complex and controversial subject, especially when it is a question of identifying different stages in the history of the Church.[3] If, in Jesus Christ, and above all in his resurrection from the dead, the eschatological longing of God's people has been satisfied, how can we explain the evident fact that history has continued with no apparent interruption? How are we to describe the day after "the last day"—and the day after that?

The letters to the Thessalonians, because of their antiquity, offer an obvious interest when we attempt to answer this question, although one not always easy to interpret. In these letters the eschatological outlook is quite apparent, and Paul always makes use of Jewish categories of thought to express himself: the faithful are waiting for the "Day of the Lord" that "will come like a thief in the night" (1 Thess 5,2). This Day is, for Paul as for the rest of the Jewish apocalyptic tradition, a time when unrepentant evildoers will experience "God's wrath," a technical term to indicate the passion of his love that can never tolerate evil (2 Thess 1,7–9). But this Day is even more the time when "the Lord Jesus" will come to bring definitive liberation to his followers (1 Thess 1,10; 2 Thess 1,7; cf. 1 Thess 5,9). It is not something, then, that believers should be afraid of; on the contrary, the apostle speaks of the *parousia* or advent of Christ as a reality that is deeply longed for, the end that gives meaning and consistency to all that comes before it (1 Thess 2,19; 3,13; 5,23; 2 Thess 1,10; 2,14). Paul even has to console the Thessalonians by explaining to them that at the Lord's coming those who are already dead will not be left behind but will rise to meet the Lord together with those who are still alive (1 Thess 4,13–18). Here, then, the apostle seems to expect the event in an imminent future. And yet no one knows the exact hour (1 Thess 5,1–2) and it would be a mistake to imagine that the Day is already here (2 Thess 2,1–12). An attitude of perseverance is necessary to live one's faith in an indifferent or hostile world; Christians must "stand firm in the Lord" (1 Thess 3,8; 2 Thess 2,15).

It would seem then that, for Paul, the eschatological longing remains unfulfilled, that Jesus' coming among us, his death and his resurrection, are not the last word God has to say. If we examine his words more closely, however, we may be inclined to modify that judgment. Chapter 5 of 1 Thess is crucial in this regard. After having explained the traditional teaching on the Day of the Lord and its uncertain character, Paul goes on to say:

But you, my brothers and sisters, are not in the darkness, for the Day to come upon you like a thief; you are all sons of the light and sons of the Day. We do not belong to the night or to the darkness. Therefore let us not fall asleep like the others, but let us remain awake and alert. (1 Thess 5,4–6)

The expression "sons of the Day" is a Semitism. It means that Christians already belong to the Day, that here and now they are walking in its light and that as a result its coming cannot catch them unawares (1 Thess 5,4). In other words, the coming Day is already present in the life of those following the lead of the Spirit, because of their acceptance of the Good News preached by Paul, because of their communion with the crucified and risen Christ. Consequently, even at this early stage, the last things are not only seen as future realities; from the first encounter with the risen Christ they are present and accessible to believers.

It is as if, for Paul, the Event of Jesus Christ—the definitive, eschatological reality—is a complex reality that surrounds us on all sides. This Event belongs to the past insofar as it is identical with the life, death and resurrection of Jesus, who was in the world as one of us. It is likewise part of the present in the work of evangelization, in the presence of the Risen Lord who creates and directs the Christian community by his Word and by his Spirit. And finally, it belongs to the future as the Day of the Lord that will mark the end of human history. In the letters to the Thessalonians, the future aspect of the Event occupies a bit more room in the apostle's thought than it does in some of his later letters, but this is primarily a question of different accents. The underlying reality is the same. The community of believers roots its existence in Jesus, who died for us (1 Thess 5,10) and rose from the dead (1 Thess 1,10); it is currently "in the Lord Jesus Christ" (1 Thess 1,1; cf. 4,16; 5,12.18; 2 Thess 1,1) and imitates his behavior (1 Thess 1,6); it lives in hope (1 Thess 4,13), looking forward to his final Coming (1 Thess 1,10) in order to be with him forever (1 Thess 4,17). The great Day, when the significance of Christ's life (his "glory") will be fully manifest, is already somehow present in the life of the faithful who walk on his way, just as it was in the earthly existence of Jesus of Nazareth. Here we are not following the linear logic of a clock or a calendar. In Jesus Christ the Day of the Lord is at hand; it comes to meet us, and already we walk in its light.

Relationships of communion

In the letters of his "mature period" written toward the end of the 50s (PHILIPPIANS, 1–2 CORINTHIANS, GALATIANS, ROMANS), Paul takes up the same themes we have just examined, developing them further. He does this first of all regarding the transmission of a new Life, involving the relationship between the apostle and Christ on the one hand, and between the apostle and the communities to which he writes on the other.

First of all, Paul constantly mentions the personal relationship which unites him to Christ and to God, the basis of his missionary activity. Even though he never met Jesus personally on earth, the risen Christ broke into his life (1 Cor 15,8), setting him apart, then calling him and sending him out (Gal 1,15ff; Rom 15,16ff). As a result he generally introduces himself at the beginning of his letters as someone "called to be an apostle" (1 Cor 1,1; Rom 1,1), and he is strongly attached to this title of apostle because it is a sign of the authenticity of the Gospel he proclaims (cf. Gal 2,5). Sometimes, notably in the epistle to the Galatians, he takes great pains to justify his ministry against the attacks of his opponents, to such an extent that he has been suspected of exalting himself to the detriment of the Jerusalem community and the Twelve. Upon closer reading, however, we can see that for Paul communion with the other apostles and the "saints" of Jerusalem is essential (e.g. Gal 1,18; 2,9; Rom 15,25ff), and he knows well that he himself is "the least of the apostles" (1 Cor 15,9). If he seems to be putting himself forward, that is in order to emphasize more strongly God's generosity towards the undeserving, the heart of his message (1 Cor 15,10; 2 Cor 12,7ff; Phil 3,4ff).

Thus Paul describes himself as someone sent by God (Gal 1,1); he received the message he brings directly from Christ (Gal 1,12). In his human weakness the power of the Holy Spirit is at work, transforming the hearts of his hearers (1 Cor 2,3–5; Rom 15,19; cf. 1 Cor 4,19f; Gal 3,2–5). Paul coins a whole series of expressions to describe, by analogy, the identity of an apostle.

They are assistants of Christ and caretakers of the mysteries of God (1 Cor 4,1), servants of God (2 Cor 6,4) or of Christ (2 Cor 11,23), slaves of Christ (Gal 1,10; Phil 1,1) or of Christians on account of Jesus (2 Cor 4,5), ambassadors of Christ (2 Cor 5,20), God's co-workers (1 Cor 3,9). Paul is a minister of Christ Jesus with the priestly duty of preaching the Gospel (Rom 15,16); he is an imitator of Christ (1 Cor 11,1). These images are taken from the most varied fields, but one thing remains constant in them all: they all express the fact that the apostle does not act in his own name but comes in place of someone else. Like every Christian and in exemplary fashion, Paul knows that he does not belong to himself (Rom 14,7–8); in his humanity Christ continues his own work (Gal 2,20). Humanly speaking, of course, he wears himself out to bring the Good News to the Gentiles (e.g. 2 Cor 11,23ff), but on a deeper level God is the one acting through him: Paul plants the seed, but God makes it grow; Paul lays the foundations, but the house is God's (1 Cor 3,6–10).

So when the apostle comes to a place to bring the Gospel, in fact God, or Christ, is the one coming to call people to holiness (1 Cor 1,2; Rom 1,7), to communion with him (1 Cor 1,9). Concretely, this takes place by means of the message which is announced and accepted (Rom 10,8ff; 1 Cor 15,1–2; Gal 1,11; Phil 1,14), above all that of the paschal mystery (1 Cor 1,17f; 2,1f). But it also involves a sharing of life, an imitation which is more a process of receptivity in trust, a kind of osmosis, than a superficial mimicry. If Paul has received the Spirit of God (1 Cor 2,12) and thus possesses the mindset (*nous*) of Christ (1 Cor 2,16), then he can propose himself as an example to be imitated by others (1 Cor 4,6.16; Phil 3,17; 4,9; cf. 1,30; Gal 4,12). In following his behavior from within, they are in fact imitating Christ (1 Cor 11,1), whose very being is the rule of life for believers (Phil 2,5; Rom 15,1–3).

The transmission of the Gospel, by preaching it and by living it out, creates new relationships of solidarity between the apostle and those he evangelizes. Paul uses several different images to express this relationship. The Corinthians, for example, are his work, the seal of his apostleship (1 Cor 9,1–2), a letter from Christ written by his efforts (2 Cor 3,2–3). They are a source of mutual pride and confidence (2 Cor 1,14; cf. Phil 2,16; 1 Thess 2,19). Writing to the Philippians, Paul uses a word difficult to translate: the faithful are "co-sharers" (*synkoinōnous*) in his grace (Phil 1,7), as well as in his trials (Phil 4,14). The same communion unites them in both suffering and joy.

Elsewhere, Paul employs the image of a family to express these relationships. He is the father who has begotten the faithful in Christ Jesus (1 Cor 4,15), and even the mother who has given birth to them in pain (Gal 4,19). They are his children (2 Cor 6,13; 12,14). In the same way, his co-worker Timothy is like a son to him (Phil 2,22). In short, deep bonds of love unite the apostle and the other believers, a love whose source is more than human: "I have you in my heart . . . I long for you all with the deep affection (lit. in the bowels) of Christ Jesus!" (Phil 1,7–8).

In our contemporary world marked by centuries of individualism and subjectivism, where the banalizing and the romanticizing of love is common currency, it is easy to misunderstand the meaning of such statements. When Paul speaks of the love uniting him to the members of a given community, this is something quite different from mere sentimentality or fine-sounding but empty words. Such phrases are a means for him to express his conviction that the principal consequence of the Gospel is the creation of brand-new human relationships, comparable in solidity and importance to those between the members of the same family. When the apostle states that he carries the faithful in his heart (Phil 1,7), he means by that that there exists between himself and his brothers and sisters in Christ a unity similar to the one between himself and the risen Christ—and this latter relationship is so deep that he can even write that Christ is living in him (Gal 2,20; Phil 1,21). When he searches the depths of his own being, then, he discovers both Christ and all those whom Christ has entrusted to him. And this communion, although it affects his subjectivity, is not merely a subjective reality. Its source lies in the death and resurrection of the Son of God and in his gift of the Holy Spirit, and not in any human feelings or desires.

For this reason, it is not surprising that instructions concerning life together occupy so much space in Paul's letters, or that divisions (1 Cor 1,10ff) and the refusal to share (1 Cor 11,17ff) are seen as the greatest of evils. On the other hand, unity born of true humility is the best way of imitating Christ (Phil 2,1ff). Although for Paul the roots of the communion among Christians

146

are interior, namely the personal relationship of faith that unites the faithful to Christ, this communion must express itself in outward behavior that even includes material sharing. So, for example, the apostle works hard to collect money to help out the Christians of Jerusalem, who are in need (1 Cor 16,1ff; 2 Cor 8–9; Rom 15,25ff). To Paul's way of thinking, such an act is not something secondary but a true expression of the mutual love which binds the Churches together, and it is rooted in the sharing of life between Christ and his followers (2 Cor 8,9; cf. Rom 15,7). Likewise, within each community people should help one another spiritually as well as materially; those whose faith is more solid have a special responsibility toward their less assured brothers and sisters (Rom 14–15). And visits between Christians, beginning with those of Paul himself, a man constantly on the road, are another important means of creating communion.

In Paul's eyes, communion is not the same thing as sterile uniformity. This communion can and must coexist with a great diversity, because it is not rooted in blind obedience or in outward conformity but in the personal call of Christ that sets a value upon the gifts of each member. To express this unity in diversity, the apostle employs the image of the human body with its different parts (1 Cor 12; Rom 12,4ff). In his writings, however, this image acquires a realism whose profundity goes far beyond that of a simple traditional analogy:

For just as the body is one and has many parts, and all the parts of the body, though there are many of them, make up only one body, the same thing is true of Christ. (1 Cor 12,12)

Instead of the expected conclusion, "the same thing is true of the Church" or ". . . of our community," Paul surprises us by these significant words: "the same thing is true of Christ." From the day of his conversion to the Gospel, Paul had realized that in the life of the Christian community the Risen Lord remains present and active (cf. Acts 9,4f; 22,7f; 26,14f). Now for a Semite, the body is not first and foremost, as it is for us, the material envelope of a human being. The word can, it is true, indicate the fact that we belong to a world menaced by fragility and death (though this notion is usually translated in Greek as "the flesh"), but it refers even more specifically to someone's *presence* in the world, to other people; it is basically a word that expresses a

147

relationship.[4] To say that we are the Body of Christ, then, is still another way for Paul to emphasize that the community of believers, animated by the Spirit of God (1 Cor 12,11.13), is the concrete continuation in history of the existence of Jesus Christ. As long as the communion is preserved, diversity cannot hurt this vocation but is rather an advantage, because it makes Christ present in a great variety of ways. If, however, the specific identity of each member or group were to become a pretext for splitting off from the rest of the Body (1 Cor 12,15ff), the essential identity of the Christian way would quickly become obscured. "Is Christ divided?" (1 Cor 1,13a).

The most excellent way

The letters of maturity of Saint Paul offer us above all a deeper examination of the way of the Lord, of how to go further on a pilgrimage of communion with God in the company of Jesus Christ. Already in the letters to the Thessalonians, we saw how much importance was given to the dimension of progress or growth in faith. Writing to the Philippians several years later, Paul describes this progress as requiring human effort, of course, but still more as an activity performed by God in human beings. He urges them to "work out your own salvation with fear and trembling" (Phil 2,12), in other words with the utmost seriousness, but he adds immediately afterwards: "for God is the one actively at work in you, in both your willing and your acting, for the sake of his saving designs" (Phil 2,13). The apostle prays for their continual growth in love (Phil 1,9), and he is sure that "the One who began in you this good work will bring it to completion until the Day of Christ Jesus" (Phil 1,6).

Similarly, Paul speaks to the Corinthians about a daily inner renewal (2 Cor 4,16) and, in a remarkable sentence, he joins the two dimensions of human growth and divine activity in Christians:

And all of us who, with faces uncovered, mirror (or: contemplate) the glory of the Lord, are transformed into the same image, from glory to glory, by the work of the Lord, who is Spirit. (2 Cor 3,18)

Because of their relationship with the risen Christ who sends them the Spirit, the faithful have God's glory shining in their hearts (2 Cor 4,6). Little by little, the light that they reflect transfigures them from within; they become the image of Christ to an ever greater degree ("from glory to glory"). This transformation occurs from within; God is the principal actor.[5] And yet not without human cooperation, since they are the ones who have to turn to the Lord so that the veil will drop (2 Cor 3,16).

Faithful to his Hebrew origins, Paul uses images of the road to describe human or divine behavior. He does this, of course, when he quotes or makes allusion to the Scriptures (e.g. Rom 3,15–17; 11,33; 2 Cor 6,16), but it is sometimes his own way of speaking as well, as when he explains to the Corinthians that Timothy will remind them of "my ways that are in Christ" (1 Cor 4,17), or that Titus and he follow the same tracks (2 Cor 12,18).

These expressions are most probably just metaphors that should not be pressed too much. We can find other indications, though, of the fact that for Paul the Christian life is a way to be followed. Could the spiritual history of his people have left him any other alternative? The apostle reflects upon the example of Abraham (Gal 3,6ff; Rom 4) and the lessons of Israel's sojourn in the wilderness (1 Cor 10). Moreover he knows that, in Christ, God has prepared for us "a more excellent way" (1 Cor 12,31). In one letter, he describes the Christian pilgrimage using the striking image of a victory parade, with Christ as the hero leading the way (2 Cor 2,14). But more often, to represent the life of faith, Paul uses the image of the *race* (1 Cor 9,24–27; Gal 2,2; 5,7; Phil 2,16; 3,12–14). The image expresses well the dynamic character of this life, as well as the constant effort required of human beings: it is important not to have "run in vain." If Christian life is a race, then what matters is to live fully in each present day, with an eye on the future. The believer is thus implicitly contrasted with men and women settled comfortably or despairingly in their routines. And yet even here, in employing the extremely "active" image of the race, the apostle never forgets that God's activity takes precedence over human effort. In one of those paradoxical statements of which he alone has the secret, Paul proclaims: " . . . I keep on going so that I may take hold [of the prize], because I myself was taken hold of by Christ Jesus" (Phil 3,12b). Being on the road is the fundamental condition of

Christians, but already at the start they have encountered the goal.

What is the course of this race? Does Paul provide us with an itinerary of this "most excellent way" he urges the readers of his letters to follow? First of all, it is a being-on-the-move under the guidance of the Holy Spirit. God has sent into the hearts of the faithful the Spirit of his Son (Gal 4,6), source of a new Life (Rom 8,11). From then on they "walk not according to the flesh but according to the Spirit" (Rom 8,4); they are led by the Spirit (Gal 5,18; Rom 8,14). The famous chapter 8 of the Letter to the Romans describes this "life according to the Spirit" contrasted with "life according to the flesh," in other words a self-centered existence, trying in vain to fashion for itself a place under the sun according to its own lights and its own efforts. For Paul, such a course is a dead-end, leading only to death (Rom 8,13). Even Christians, if they do not grow in faith, run the risk of living in this way; by their disputes and their spirit of jealousy and rivalry they are "of the flesh and walk in a merely human manner" (1 Cor 3,1–4). Since the Spirit is the true wellspring of their life, it is up to them to walk according to the Spirit (Gal 5,25; cf. 5,16). Then they will bear the fruits of the Spirit: joy, peace, goodness, and many others (Gal 5,22). And above all the fruit of *agape*, charity or Christian love, the synthesis and fulfillment of the Torah (Gal 5,14). In a word, the "most excellent way" is the way of love (1 Cor 13; cf. Eph 5,2).

Dead and risen with Christ

In the great letters of Saint Paul, the Christian way, the way of love, tends to become more and more identified with the *paschal mystery*, with Jesus' Passover from death to new life. The center of the Good News proclaimed by Paul is the crucified Christ, God's foolishness wiser than human wisdom and God's weakness stronger than human strength (1 Cor 1,17ff). Christ, "handed over for our faults and raised up for our justification" (Rom 4,25), is the entrance-way to the new life for believers (Rom 5,2).

But Paul goes still further. For him, the paschal mystery, the death and resurrection of Christ, is not only the source of grace; it is its content as well. In other words, what God gives in sending his Son among us is above all the possibility of taking part in the Son's pilgrimage from death to eternal life, to life in communion. Thus the paschal journey of Christ is both source and model of the Christian life; it provides the essential contours of the Way traced out by God at the heart of human history.

For believers, this Way begins simultaneously with the beginning of the life of faith in baptism. Paul describes baptism as a death and an entrance into a new life:

> We have therefore been buried with [Christ] by baptism into death so that, just as Christ was raised from the dead by the glory of the Father, we too might walk in the newness of life. (Rom 6,4)

Being Christian means having been crucified with Christ (Gal 2,19; cf. 5,24; 6,14) in order to live a life rooted in him (Gal 2,20; cf. Rom 6,11; Phil 1,21), in order to belong henceforth to him alone, the Risen Lord (Rom 7,4; cf. 14,8; 1 Cor 3,23; 6,19). For us, born in a civilization where most Christians have been baptized as children, these phrases might sound like impressive but rather unreal images. For the first Christians, however, as well as for a substantial part of the Church still today, they describe quite accurately an existential reality that is both demanding and joyful. Being baptized meant leaving behind a whole world with its values, its habits and its relationships, in order to join a community that led a drastically different life, a full life but one at the same time often insecure, and even hazardous, involving an uncertain future from a human point of view. In short, it meant risking one's life for the sake of Christ. Those of us who have been "born Christian" need to meditate on the radical significance of our baptism, if we are not to reduce the paschal pilgrimage to a simple sociological category.

Paul describes baptism, the starting-point and the recapitulation of the Christian life, as our participation in the Lord's saving death. Concretely, this means that Christians will not fail to experience trials, sufferings that they will view as an existential sharing in the cross of Christ. For Paul, there is nothing theoretical about this statement. He experiences its truth daily as he lives out his calling:

We always carry around in our bodies the dying of Jesus, so that the life of Jesus may be revealed as well in our bodies. For we, though alive, are always being handed over to death for the sake of Jesus, so that the life of Jesus as well may be revealed in our mortal flesh. (2 Cor 4,10–11)

Paul explains to the Philippians that it is a great gift to suffer for Christ (Phil 1,29–30), and he even writes to the Romans that "we boast about our tribulations" (Rom 5,3). Such phrases have nothing morbid about them. Paul is not praising suffering as such, but only suffering as a road to resurrection, as a sharing in the definitive liberation of the entire universe in Christ (cf. Rom 8,18ff). This liberation is not only a future reality: writing to the Corinthians (2 Cor 1,3–11; 4,8–12), Paul celebrates the mysterious dialectic of troubles and consolations already at work in his own existence and that of the community. He views this as the paschal mystery constantly being made present in his life. The important thing in all this is to follow Christ; it is not *suffering*, but suffering-*with-him* that is the key. The well-known hymn that the apostle reproduces in his letter to the Philippians (Phil 2,6–11) reveals the authentic meaning of this *kenosis* or self-emptying of Jesus by describing it as a consequence of divine generosity. Precisely because he was "of divine state," Christ did not seek to profit from what he had but rather to share it as much as possible by going down to take the very last place. Once again, love is the key that solves the riddle.

The cross of Christ is thus for Paul a permanent dimension of the life of believers. As for our current participation in the resurrection of Christ, the apostle expresses himself in a more nuanced manner. He emphasizes at times the present aspect and at times the future aspect of this reality. When he speaks of baptism as a dying with Christ, the new life of Christians appears to be a present reality in his thought (Rom 6,4), but our resurrection is qualified by a future verb (Rom 6,5: "will be"). Likewise, in 1 Cor 6,14 (at least in the most probable reading), our resurrection is seen as something still to come. In another passage, however, Paul speaks of Christians as "living beings [returned] from death" (Rom 6,13). At this stage of his reflection, it seems that Paul hesitates to use the word "resurrection" (or "glorification," cf. Rom 8,17) to refer to the present state of Christians, perhaps in part so as not to offer support to extremists who claimed already to have attained perfection in a manner similar to devotees of the Hellenistic mystery religions.

Confronted with such a reduction of faith, Paul stresses the future dimension of the Gospel, the dimension of waiting in hope, just as at another time, when he was faced with people who could not see the newness of the Gospel over against its Jewish background, he placed the accent on Christ as already the fulfillment of the Torah (cf. Rom 10,4). It is true that in Christ's coming all the divine promises have been fulfilled (2 Cor 1,20); the end of the ages (1 Cor 10,11) or the fullness of time (Gal 4,4) has arrived. Still, this fullness is only accessible to us in hope (Rom 5,5; 8,24f). Already at present we possess the Spirit as "first-fruits" (Rom 8,23), as a "seal" (2 Cor 1,22; cf. Eph 4,30; 1,13), as a "deposit" or "down payment" (2 Cor 1,22; 5,5; cf. Eph 1,14) of a future fulfillment.

The apostle employs a great diversity of expressions to express the eschatological horizon of his faith. He is longing for the "Day of Christ" (1 Cor 1,8; 2 Cor 1,14; Phil 1,6.10; 2,16) or "of the Lord" (1 Cor 5,5), sometimes simply called "the Day" (1 Cor 3,13; cf. Rom 13,12). Does Paul identify this Day with Judgment Day (Rom 2,5.16) and God's judgment seat (Rom 14,10)? It seems so (cf. 1 Cor 4,4f; 2 Cor 5,10), even though his choice of expressions seems to be determined above all by the context; he is not trying to set up a rigorous system in this area. Elsewhere, he speaks of the revealing (1 Cor 1,7; cf. Rom 8,18–19; 16,25) or the advent (*parousia*, 1 Cor 15,23) of Christ, of his coming (1 Cor 4,5; 11,26; cf. 13,10; Phil 3,20), of a face-to-face meeting (1 Cor 13,12). Another cluster of images concerns primarily the fact of our resurrection (1 Cor 15), described by Paul as a transfiguration of our bodies (1 Cor 15,51–52; Phil 3,21) or as their being clothed in immortality (1 Cor 15,53–54; 2 Cor 5,1–5).

The very diversity of these images is proof that, for the apostle, the important thing is not to provide detailed, empirical images of a future necessarily far beyond anything human beings can conceive (cf. 1 Cor 2,9). Paul has nothing in common with a visionary attempting to scrutinize the mysteries of God. His center of gravity is located elsewhere, in the present moment. What concerns him most is his calling to bring the Good News to the Gentiles, to foster the birth and growth of local Christian communities. He only speculates about future realities when he is obliged to deal with manifest errors, and even then, he says just enough to close off certain avenues of thought and to bring his readers back to the essentials of the faith that he received and handed on to them (see e.g. 1 Cor 15).

The images of the absolute future used by Paul in his letters have an even deeper justification as well: they are there to help believers to live in the present in conformity with the Gospel message. This is clearly visible from some lines written by Paul to the Christians of Corinth:

> I am telling you, my brothers, the time is running out. From now on, those who have a wife should live as if they had none; those who are weeping, as if they were not weeping; those who are joyful, as if they were not joyful; those who make purchases, as if they had no possessions; those who are using the world, as if they were not really making use of it. For the world as we know it is passing away. (1 Cor 7,29–31)

These sentences give us the basis of Christian morality. To live in the light of the coming Day means to be *in* the world without being *of* the world (cf. John 17,14ff), witnessing to a different future. While taking part in the life of the human family, becoming "all things to all people" (1 Cor 9,19–23), rejoicing with those who are happy and weeping with those who are sad (Rom 12,15), those who are longing for Christ know that their true center is elsewhere. Their homeland is in heaven (Phil 3,20), and this gives them a certain freedom with respect to the pressures and the illusions of a world closed in upon itself. Paradoxically, the fact of living in the light of another reality gives believers the distance necessary in order to be closer to others here and now (cf. 1 Cor 9,19; Gal 5,13). They are "wide awake" (1 Thess 5,6), basically joyful even in the midst of the worries and the troubles of the world (Phil 4,4–7). In short, far from taking our attention away from the problems of this world, Christian eschatology provides us with what we need to confront these problems truly. It enables us to live authentically, as pilgrims, in the midst of our human condition.

Paul shows us the relationship between the paschal mystery lived out by Jesus, our own daily behavior and our longing for fulfillment in an extremely significant passage in which he takes up once again the image of the race:

154

[I want] to know [Christ], and experience the power of his resurrection and communion in his sufferings, becoming like him in his death so that if possible I might attain the resurrection from the dead. Not that I have already reached the goal or already become perfect, but I keep going in order to take hold, since I myself was taken hold of by Christ Jesus. (Phil 3,10–12)

Here we can see to what extent the Christian pilgrimage differs from the outward imitation of a model. For the apostle, everything begins with his communion with the Risen Lord, a communion that infuses new energy into his life. It gives him the strength for com-passion, to suffer with Christ, and in this way to live out in his own existence the mystery of dying-and-rising, with his final resurrection at the end of the road. "Taken hold of" by Christ, he sets out on a journey toward a definitive encounter with him. The presence of the Holy Spirit in believers is a source of "dissatisfaction," a motive force that propels them toward a fulfillment (Rom 8,23). Already we possess, or rather, we are possessed (Phil 3,12b), but the gift placed by God in our hands is the gift of a Way. Although humanly speaking it is a paradox, the only possibility to be perfect, for a Christian, is to be on the road (Phil 3,12a.15), following the way of the Lord, celebrating "the Lord's Passover" by living it out.

Contemplating the mystery

When we go from the great letters of Saint Paul to his so-called "letters of captivity," COLOSSIANS and EPHESIANS, the outlook is not quite the same. For this reason, many Scripture scholars have expressed doubts about the Pauline origin of these two letters, or at least of Ephesians. Although the main themes of the apostle remain present, everything is set in the context of the contemplation of the *mystery* (Col 1,26.27; 2,2; Eph 1,9; 3,3–5.9; 5,32; 6.19), in other words God's all-encompassing intention for the universe, "the mystery of [God's] will, according to his good pleasure, which he set out ahead of time in [Jesus Christ], to be worked out in stages as the times reached their fulfillment" (Eph 1,9b-10a). The goal of this divine plan is the *reconciliation* (Col 1,20) or *recapitulation* (Eph 1,10) of all things in Christ, and this becomes a concrete reality in the existence of the Church, where Jews and Gentiles together form "one new Humanity" (*anthropos*, Eph 2,15; cf. Col 3,9–11), a perfect or fully mature Man (*anēr*, Eph 4,13), God's family (Eph 2,19; cf. 3,6).

The accent is thus placed on what is already acquired, on Christ's victory, by the gift of his life ("his blood," Col 1,20; Eph 1,7; 2,13), over all the powers of evil in the world (Col 2,15; cf. Eph 6,12), notably the forces of division and hostility (Eph 2,14). So, for example, we have already been "liberated from the power of darkness and transferred into the Kingdom of the Son he loves" (Col 1,13). Here, as opposed to the other Pauline letters, the author does not hesitate to speak of the resurrection— and even of life in heaven—as a reality already present for believers (Col 2,12; 3,1; Eph 2,6). This goes very far in the direction of "realized eschatology," and it could be feared that the dynamic images of growth and progress, so important in the rest of Paul's writings, might be neglected or forgotten here.

A closer reading, however, will convince us that the dimension of Christianity as a way is still part of the outlook of these letters, especially of Colossians. Once again, although the essential has already been given, it was not given as a static conclusion but as a principle of growth. The Gospel "which reached you" is bearing fruit and growing all over the world (Col 1,6), in part through the ministry of Paul himself (Col 1,28–29), by his mission to "bring to fulfillment the Word of God" (Col 1,25). This Word communicates a "hope set aside for you in the heavens" (Col 1,5; cf. 1,23.27; Eph 1,18), and believers, because of the presence in them of the Holy Spirit, already possess this hope in the bud (Eph 1,13–14). Risen with Christ, the faithful are still looking forward to the time when they will be "manifested" with him in glory (Col 3,1–4). While celebrating the wonders already accomplished by Christ's coming and his pilgrimage back to the Father, the author keeps his eyes on a final fulfillment which is not yet complete.

This dialectic becomes still more evident when we go from the indicative to the imperative, from the description of the mystery of salvation to its consequences for the life of the faithful. The latter dimension involves our living out individually and communally what God has already made possible in the universe and in history by sending his Son. To put it briefly, it is a question of "walking in a manner worthy of the Lord" (Col 1,10; cf. 1 Thess 2,12), or of "walking in Christ Jesus the Lord as you received him" (Col 2,6). This is a consequence of a change of heart: the old roads that lead nowhere are left behind (Col 3,7; Eph 4,17) so that we may walk as children of light (Eph 5,8; cf. 1 Thess 5,5), in love (Eph 5,2), by imitating God (Eph 5,1). And so, for example, the apostle can pray that the faithful may come to know fully the will of God (Col 1,9; Eph 1,17–18) and discover all the dimensions of his unfathomable love (Eph 3,14–19). The power of this love in them will keep them faithful and joyful (Col 1,11); it is "able to do much, much more than anything we can ask for or conceive" (Eph 3,20b).

In general, however, these two letters prefer other images to metaphors of the road. First of all, there is that of *changing clothes*, more meaningful in the ancient world where people's garb was a clear indication of their station, of their identity. By their baptism and entry into the communion of saints (cf. Col 1,2.4.12.22; Eph 1,1.4 etc.), the Church, Christians have "taken off the old self with its practices and have put on the new one, which is being renewed in knowledge in line with the image of its creator" (Col 3,9b-10). In their new identity as members of Christ's Body, the faithful experience a perpetual renewal of their understanding and acting. Ephesians, in a similar phrase, places the accent on human activity: believers should leave behind their former way of life, that of the "old humanity," in order to be renewed and to put on "the new humanity" (Eph 4,22–24). Nevertheless, the author quickly adds that this new humanity is "created according to God"; it is not merely the fruit of human activity but a consequence of God's creative energy liberated in the resurrection of Jesus Christ (cf. Eph 1,19–20).

The image of changing clothes has paschal overtones, and the Christian pilgrimage as a participation in the death and resurrection of Christ leaves its mark here too. In his own ministry, the apostle "completes in [his] flesh what is lacking in the tribulations of Christ for his Body, which is the Church" (Col 1,24b). This fills him with the joy of Easter in the midst of his sufferings (Col 1,24a; cf. Eph 3,13). Likewise, Christians "have died with Christ to the elements of the world" (Col 2,20; cf. Eph 2,1), and in their turn they must "put to death [their] earthly attachments" and "seek the things above" (Col 3,5.1–2). This dying and rising occurs in an exemplary fashion in *forgiveness*. In constantly crossing over, in the footsteps of Christ (Col 3,13; Eph 4,32), from alienation and hostility to unity and love, Christians discover that peace which is not passivity (for the life of faith is a spiritual combat, Eph 6,10ff) but rather the fullness of a communion (Col 3,15; Eph 2,14–18).

And finally, the letters of captivity explain the Christian way above all by employing the image of *the growth of the body*. Ephesians expresses perfectly the relationship between Christ's pilgrimage and that of his followers by some words difficult to understand at first reading: Christians must "grow up in all respects into him who is the Head, Christ" (Eph 4,15). To grasp the point of the image, we must realize that here the head does not connote supremacy or sovereignty, as it does for us in the West (Latin *caput*, cf. English *captain, chief*). For the Greek mentality, the head does not govern the body, but rather it is the starting-point for the whole body as well as the body in miniature, a kind of microcosm or re-*capit*-ulation.[6] In Colossians, therefore, Christ is "the Head of the Body, that is the Church" because he is "the Beginning (*archē*[7]), the Firstborn from among the dead," the one in whom all fullness dwells (Col 1,18–19). From the Head, "the whole Body, receiving by means of its joints and ligaments nourishment and cohesion, grows up as God causes it to grow" (Col 2,19).

To say that God made Christ "Head over the Church" (Eph 1,22f) is equivalent to saying that, by his resurrection, Christ is the starting-point of a new, reconciled humanity; he is a kind of second Adam (cf. Rom 5,12ff; 1 Cor 15,20–22). In the Head the whole Body is already virtually present, and yet this Body must grow and attain full maturity. From the Head, all the gifts necessary for the building up of the Body flow (Eph 4,7–12), but these gifts must be put to use in the unity of Christian love (Eph 4,1–6). This explains why, in these two letters, the way of the Lord is expressed primarily in terms of the growth or building up of the Body of Christ,

> until we all attain unity in faith and in the knowledge of the Son of God, becoming the perfect Man, fully mature with the fullness of Christ. (Eph 4,13)

This "perfect Man, fully mature," the *totus Christus*, Christ together with his worldwide Body, is the ultimate reality (cf. Col 2,17), the climax of God's loving designs from the very beginning (Eph 1,9–10). The contemplation of this universal mystery gives meaning and consistency to every personal pilgrimage in the company of Jesus Christ.

Questions for Reflection

1. The letters of Saint Paul present faith not as ideas or theories about God but as the transmission of a new Life. Personally, from where did I receive this Life? How do I transmit it to others?

2. Paul uses the expression "sons of light, sons of the Day" (1 Thess 5,5) to describe Christians. In this way he emphasizes the fact that they do not follow the values and patterns of a world doomed to disappear but that they already live in the light of a different future, of God's presence in fullness among us. Concretely, what does this expression mean for our way of life, for our life-style?

3. For the apostle, the Christian life is essentially a life of communion with God that is translated into relationships of communion, of community, between women and men whose life has been transformed by Christ. How can we root our existence in this double communion? Does my own relationship with God lead me to look for communion with all people, beginning with those who, like me, bear the name of Christ? What gestures of solidarity and sharing can we accomplish in our own situations? How can we go beyond our differences and discover a common belonging?

4. What is the difference between unanimity and uniformity, between diversity and division in the Christian community? How does the Pauline image of the body and its parts (1 Cor 12) help us to understand the structure of the Christian community and the relationship between unity and diversity?

5. Why does Paul employ the image of a *race* (1 Cor 9,24–27; Phil 3,12–14) to describe the life of faith? What does he mean by describing baptism (Rom 6,4), or even the whole of a Christian's life (Gal 2,19–20; Rom 6,11; 7,4; 2 Cor 4,10–11), as a participation in the death and the resurrection of Christ?

6. According to Colossians and Ephesians, the goal of God's plan is the reconciliation (Col 1,20) or recapitulation (Eph 1,10) of the universe in Christ, the creation of one new Humanity (Eph 2,15; cf. Col 3,9–11). How does this statement enable us to determine our priorities as believers? What consequences does it have for the role of the Church in the world?

Notes

[1]It should be mentioned that, according to some scholars, 2 Thess does not belong here chronologically. Some even consider it a later imitation of Saint Paul and not an authentic Pauline letter. Whatever the value of this hypothesis, the argument of this chapter would not be substantially modified.

[2]At the same time, Christian imitation is something far more profound than the simple attempt to copy an exterior model. See the enlightening article of David Stanley, "Imitation in Paul's Letters: Its Significance for His Relationship to Jesus and to His Own Christian Foundations" in Peter Richardson & John C. Hurd (eds.), *From Jesus to Paul: Studies in Honour of Francis Wright Beare* (Waterloo, Ont., Canada: Wilfrid Laurier Univ. Press, 1984), pp. 127–141.

[3]On this topic see Jörg Baumgarten, *Paulus und die Apokalyptik: Die Auslegung apokalyptischen Überlieferungen in den echten Paulusbriefen* (Neukirchener Verlag, 1975). The author shows that, for the apostle, mythological or apocalyptic speculation on the "end of the world" is relatively unimportant. Moreover, he counsels against any attempt to establish a "theory of evolution" to interpret Paul's eschatological thinking, particularly based on a notion such as "the expectation of an imminent end (*Nah-Erwartung*)." See especially pp. 198–226, 236–238.

[4]For John A.T. Robinson, *The Body: A Study in Pauline Theology* (Chicago: Henry Regnery Co., 1952), the notion of the body is the cornerstone of Pauline theology. He stresses the fact that the Hebrew language has no specific word for body, and that the same word, *bāsār*, is translated in Greek both by *sarx* ("flesh") and by *sōma* ("body"). If the term *sarx* emphasizes the perishable and transitory nature of creation, the word *sōma* "stands for man, in the solidarity of creation, as made for God" (p. 31). In any event, for the Hebrews, "the locus of individuation was not found at this point . . . The flesh-body was not what partitioned a man off from his neighbour; it was rather what bound him in the bundle of life with all men and nature, so that he could never make his unique answer to God as an isolated individual . . ." (p. 15).

[5]Translating *katoptrizomai* as "to contemplate" and not "to mirror," which fits less well with the context, would introduce a slightly more active nuance but would not alter the fundamental meaning of the passage.

[6]On this question, see Francis Grob, "L'image du corps et de la tête dans l'Epître aux Ephésiens," *Etudes Théologiques et Religieuses* 1983–84 (vol. 58), pp. 491–500.

[7]It is interesting that the Greek word *archē* has the two meanings "beginning, origin" and "sovereignty." There seems to be a rather obvious semantic shift from the notion of being first to that of being the ruler. Cf. the English words "to lead," "prince."

SEVEN

Pilgrims and Strangers

The apostolic letters that follow the Pauline corpus do not add much to our understanding of faith as a pilgrimage. With two exceptions, the authors make use of the same images of the road that we have already examined, and the theme does not represent a cornerstone of their reflection. So, for example, the letters of John encourage the faithful to walk in the light and not in the darkness (1 John 1,6–7; 2,11), to walk in the truth (2 John 4; 3 John 3; 4; cf. 2 John 6) in the steps of Christ (1 John 2,6). John speaks of Christian life as a passover from death to life, shown by the love that unites the members of the community (1 John 3,14).

Likewise, Paul's letters to Timothy speak of the fate of those who have wandered away from the faith (1 Tim 1,6.19; 6,10.21; 2 Tim 2,18; 4,4), and he exhorts his disciple to "pursue righteousness, piety, faith, love, patience and gentleness" (1 Tim 6,11; cf. 2 Tim 2,22). For his part, the apostle has "finished his race" (2 Tim 4,7). The letters of James and Jude contain some Semitisms incorporating the vocabulary of the road (e.g. James 1,8.11; Jude 11), and Second Peter offers us a marvelous description of the Christian life as "the way of truth" (2 Peter 2,2), although some would see this only as a Semitism signifying "the right way to live" as contrasted to the false wisdom of his opponents.

There is, however, one book of the New Testament that provides an extremely well developed vision of the way of Christ and of believers. This book is known as the Epistle to the HEBREWS, although it is not, strictly speaking, a letter. The work is in fact a kind of homily or treatise meant to encourage its audience and to help them to grow in faith by giving them the advanced teaching meant for disciples who are no longer beginners (Heb 6,1). With a great deal of sophistication the unknown author awakens the minds of his hearers to the essentials of the Christian pilgrimage, explaining to them what it means to live as followers of Jesus, the one who goes before them on the road and who clears the way for them.

Jesus, our high priest

The Epistle to the Hebrews is neither a true letter nor a gospel. To describe the stages of Jesus' career, the author prefers to use, not historical recollections, but categories taken from the Hebrew Scriptures, especially the Psalms. This procedure allows him to express more clearly the unity of God's designs over and above the movement from the "first" to the "second" covenant (cf. Heb 8,7ff), and makes the fundamental contours of the way of the Lord stand out more clearly. In short, here we are dealing with an authentic theology, a synthetic presentation of the Christian pilgrimage rich in consequences for belief.

An important image used in Hebrews to characterize Jesus comes from Psalm 110, a portrait of the Messiah who sits at God's right hand and who is "a priest forever according to the order of Melchizedek" (Ps 110,4b), thus combining in himself the two offices of king and priest. Almost every time that the epistle mentions the resurrection-exaltation of Christ, it is done by means of the metaphor of enthronement (1,3; 8,1; 10,12; 12,2), or the related image of the crossing of or entry into the heavens (4,14; 7,26; 9,24), whose connection with the figure of the high priest entering the sanctuary will shortly become evident (cf. also 6,20; 9,12; 10, 20).

In this respect, the first title given by this author to Jesus is that of *the Son,* a term which has messianic (1,5; 5,5; cf. Ps 2,7) and thus, in the light of Psalm 110, priestly (5,6; 4,14) overtones. Although this name is bestowed on him only at his enthronement-resurrection, at the end of his career (1,4–6), it expresses the fundamental and permanent truth of his being. To employ a favorite image of Hebrews, the fulfillment consists in the fact that the heir finally comes into his inheritance (cf. 1,2.4).

The first verses of the epistle (1,1–4) trace the way of Christ in a long and pregnant sentence that has been called "the most perfect Greek phrase in the New Testament."[1] Rooting himself in the Wisdom tradition of Judaism, the author presents the Son as co-creator, as a mediator between God and the created universe. This pre-existent being must then accomplish "the cleansing of sins" before being exalted and publicly acclaimed as God's Son: God presents him as his firstborn to receive the homage of the entire inhabited world (*oikoumenē*), which in this context probably means the world that has been cleansed, the world to come (1,6; cf. 2,5). Jesus' mission thus describes a trajectory of descent and ascent that parallels other New Testament passages such as the famous hymn of the letter to the Philippians (Phil 2,6–11) and the gospel according to Saint John (see ch. IV). But the beginning of Hebrews adds a historical perspective to this: the Son's coming is the definitive culmination of a whole series of acts of divine revelation (1,1–2).

An identical two-pronged structure reappears later. The text speaks of "Jesus who . . . endured a cross . . . and then took his seat at the right of God's throne" (12,2b). Similarly, in a commentary on Psalm 8, the life, death and resurrection of Jesus are described in terms of his lowering himself, being crowned and being made Lord of the universe (2,5–9). The main interest of this last passage lies in its application to Jesus of a psalm describing the vocation of human beings in general. For Hebrews, Christ, although he is the Son of God, is thus "the son of man" par excellence; he recapitulates in himself the calling of the whole human race. This is the same intuition expressed in Colossians and Ephesians by the term "Head" (cf. p. 158), whereas Hebrews prefers expressions such as "leader, guide" (*archēgos* 2,10; 12,2) or "precursor, forerunner" (*prodromos* 6,20) to describe the relationship between the Son and "the many sons" (2,10), in other words the human family called to share in God's own life.

What we have seen up to now gives us scattered elements for understanding the way of Christ according to the epistle to the Hebrews, but the keystone is still missing. This keystone is mentioned first of all in 2,17: Christ must "become like his brothers in all things, in order to become a compassionate and accredited (or: faithful) *high priest* in their relation with God, so as to make atonement for the sins of the people." For Hebrews, Jesus Christ is above all else the true high priest; this is the notion that will enable us to comprehend fully his identity and his mission.

"A high priest . . . to make atonement for the sins of the people." Since the return from the Babylonian captivity, for a Jewish community that had no political autonomy, the head of one of the principal priestly families became the symbol of the nation's unity and was given the title "high (lit. chief or first) priest." In addition, one of the most important festivals of the Jewish calendar was (and is) *Yom Kippur*, the Day of Atonement. A yearly celebration of God's forgiveness, Yom Kippur was the only day of the year when the high priest, after having offered sacrifices for his own sins and those of the people, passed through the curtain and entered the most sacred part of the Temple ("the Holy of Holies"). Once within, he offered incense and sprinkled with blood the "propitiatory" or cover of the Ark (Lev 16), acts which symbolized a renewed communion with the Lord despite the faults of the people.

For the author of Hebrews, Jesus, the Son of God, is the only one really able to bring us God's forgiveness and so to re-establish to the full a communion between God and humanity. He is, therefore, the true high priest, "compassionate and accredited . . . holy, innocent, unspotted, completely set apart from sinners, lifted up high above the heavens" (2,17; 7,26). The road he follows is described in terms of a Yom Kippur liturgy, or to put it another way, his death and resurrection accomplish in a true and definitive fashion something of which the Temple liturgy was only a "copy" (*hypodeigma*, 8,5; 9,23), a "figure" (*parabolē*, 9,9), a "foreshadowing" or "sketch" (*skia*, 8,5; 10,1) meant to prepare people's minds to receive the truth.

But before he can bring us the forgiveness of sins, the Son has to take upon himself the role of high priest and be accredited. For Hebrews, this means that he must enter the world and become a human being like us. What will later be called the incarnation is thus seen here to have a saving purpose; it makes possible Jesus' death and resurrection for us, in other words his career as high priest. Once again we meet the descent-ascent schema: Jesus is the "apostle (the one sent out) and the high priest whom we confess" (3,1); he comes into the world to do God's will with infinitely more success than all the sacrifices of the cult he replaces (10,5–10; cf. Ps 40). Hebrews explains in great detail why it was necessary for Christ to be a human being in order to save humanity. The sanctifier and those sanctified must have a similar background (2,11); "because he went through the trial himself, he is able to help those whose faith is being tried" (2,18).

Jesus had to experience death for us (2,9); for us he had to imprint in his own flesh the attitude of obedient trust in his Father even in the depths of the night (5,8–9). A compassionate high priest (4,15; 5,2), he was able to liberate us as someone who suffered with and for us. The salvation he offers is thus at the opposite extreme from a condescension from on high, since it is the fruit of an authentic solidarity, a sharing of our misery. In Jesus Christ, the way of the Lord reaches the lowest point of the human condition, and consequently, no one will ever again be placed too low to find it.

In ancient Israel, the priesthood was exercised by men from the tribe of Levi. Jesus, as a descendant of David, was of the tribe of Judah (7,13–14). This would seem to be a fundamental obstacle to the recognition by the Jewish people of his identity as the true high priest. Hebrews is fully aware of this difficulty, as one might expect, and the solution found solves the problem at hand as well as illuminating the whole question of the relationship between the Gospel and the Torah. Remember that, according to Psalm 110, the Messiah is a "priest according to the order of Melchizedek." Now Melchizedek, the King of Salem, is a figure who comes before and outside of the economy of Israel, "with no father, no mother, no genealogy, with no beginning to his days nor end to his life . . ." (7,3). Because of this, he is a particularly apt figure of the Son of God (cf. 7,3b).

The argument of Hebrews rests on the relationship between Melchizedek and Abraham, recounted in chapter 14 of the Book of Genesis. After his victorious campaign against the Canaanite kings, the patriarch gives a tenth of all his booty to the priest-king and receives his blessing. In Abraham, their father, it is thus as if the entire people of Israel—including Aaron, Levi and all the priests and Levites who descended from them—acknowledged a superior priesthood (7,1ff). In this way, far ahead of time, the limits of the Levitical priesthood were already traced out, and indeed the limits of the Law of Moses as a whole (7,12.18–19). Although he apparently came later, Christ was in fact first: he is that "priest according to the order of Melchizedek" to whom God commits himself by a formal oath (7,17.20–22). The covenant he guarantees is thus a better one (7,22; 8,6), and even an everlasting one (13,20). Christ is "the mediator of a new covenant" (9,15; 12,24; cf. 8,8.13), but this does not imply a kind of afterthought on God's part; the example of Melchizedek bears witness to the fact that this intention is even older than the existence of God's people. The economy of the Torah of Moses is surrounded on all sides by the economy of the Son, a better and superior one. The relationship between the two is like that between a house and its builder, or between a servant of the family and the son (3,1–6), master of the household (3,6; 10,21).

A cosmic liturgy of reconciliation

Let us now attempt to examine more closely, in the epistle to the Hebrews, the way of Christ by which he inaugurates this new and better covenant "once and for all." In other words, how did Jesus, our high priest, celebrate that definitive Yom Kippur liturgy that fulfilled and replaced all the rites of the former economy by establishing an unbreakable communion between God and humanity?[2]

We have seen that the liturgy of the Day of Atonement took place in two successive stages. First of all, in the outer sanctuary area, the high priest sacrificed goats and rams for himself and for the people. Christ, for his part, "did this once and for all by offering himself" (7,27; cf. 9,14.28a; 10,10). In other words, Christ's sacrifice was the gift of his own life out of love for us, a gift expressed in every moment of his life on earth but recapitulated and ratified by his death on Calvary. By giving his own self in this way (his "blood"), the Son offered a more excellent sacrifice (9,23), a unique sacrifice (10,12), the only one able to obtain forgiveness (9,9; 10,1.4.11) and to establish a new covenant (9,15). As a result, all the sacrifices of the old economy have lost their reason for being (3,10; 10.18).

In our day, the language of sacrifice is not highly appreciated by many Christians. On the one hand, in everyday speech the word has taken on strong moralistic and negative connotations. It has come to mean, more or less, "doing out of a sense of duty what one would rather not do." On the other hand, where the original meaning of the word still prevails, people are repelled by the bloody side of the act: how can such an act of violence against a victim (another word from the same semantic field!) be reconciled with our Gospel of love?

To these objections a double response can be given. First of all, even apart from Christ, in ancient Israel or in other religions, it is inaccurate to claim that the element of destruction represents the essential aspect of a sacrifice. The principal inspiration for the act seems to be the desire to create or to keep up good relations with a divinity by giving a gift. To accomplish this, a particularly desirable object or being is removed from the everyday, profane world and set aside for the god or goddess. And since there are not a thousand different ways of symbolizing the giving of something to an invisible divine being, the animal, plant or product is generally made to disappear in one way or another: the wine is poured out, the fruit or grain is burnt, the lamb is eaten, and so on. Now it is certainly possible to maintain, and with reason, that in the course of the ages, other less honorable elements, due to the waywardness of human beings and their often erroneous manner of conceiving the divine, may have grafted themselves on to the institution of sacrifice. Nonetheless, the basic significance of the practice seems to have been an exchange of gifts for the purpose of creating or reinforcing a relationship.

In the second place, in the case of Christ, the human reality of sacrifice is transfigured, that is, both purified of all ambiguities and perversions and given a new and higher meaning. For example, if we apply the language of sacrifice to Christ, we have to say that he is both the *priest* and the *victim* of his sacrifice: he gives himself. This is a unique situation, and here, the element of violence is thus even less present than usual. It is not a constitutive element of the act. We must not be misled by fixing our gaze on the horrible torture of the crucifixion. In fact, the activity of his executioners gave Jesus the outward occasion for making a total gift of himself, but it in no way constituted that gift. Put another way, the Roman and Jewish authorities who were responsible for Jesus' death had no authentic desire to offer homage to God by giving God a particularly desirable gift. What constituted the sacrifice of Christ was rather his infinite *love* for the Father and for humanity, his deliberate decision to give his life to the very end, to consent to any form of suffering so as to become closer to his brothers and sisters. Saint John understood this perfectly when he reported the following words of Jesus:

> That is why the Father loves me,
> because I lay down my life,
> in order to take it up again.
> No one takes it from me;
> I lay it down of my own accord.
> I have authority to lay it down
> and I have authority to take it up again;
> this is the commandment I received from my Father.
> (John 10,17–18; cf. 18,10–11; Matt 26.52–54)

These words indicate another reason why Christ's sacrifice is different from any other. In the person of the Son, in fact it is the Father (his love, his commandment) who is giving himself. Before being a gift made by a human being to God, Christ's sacrifice is the act of God who lowers himself out of love to save the human race. In Jesus Christ, God gives himself to human beings so that human beings can give themselves to God.

In addition to the vocabulary of sacrifice, Hebrews uses another language to speak of this first dimension of Christ's pilgrimage. On the Day of Atonement, the high priest passes through the first tent on his way to the Holy of Holies. "Christ, however, arriving on the scene as the high priest of the good things to come, through the greater and more perfect tent not made by human hands, that is, not of this creation . . . entered the sanctuary once and for all . . ." (9,11–12). The verb translated by "arriving on the scene" "is more evocative of Christ's arrival than the simple *genomenos*, because the papyruses give it the connotation of arriving home, or of presenting oneself before the Judge to be heard, and finally 'to come back, return'."[3] Whether this "greater and more perfect tent" is the heavens (cf. 9,24; 4,14; 8,2) above which Jesus was raised by his death (7,26), or the tent of his body[4] (Mark 14,58; John 2,13–22), the meaning is practically the same: the earthly career of the Son of God, his coming into the world, his life and his death are a crossing, a passing through to open a road.

At this point we move, almost imperceptibly, to the second phase of the cosmic liturgy. The Jewish high priest went behind the curtain and brought the blood of the victims into the Holy of Holies. Jesus, for his part, "with his own blood" (9,12), that is, the life he had given, "entered . . . into heaven itself" (9,24). He took his place at God's right hand (1,3; 8,1; 10,12; 12,2) where he remains alive forever as an intercessor (7,24–25). On account of his resurrection-exaltation, his life with God, Christ is able to acquire for us an everlasting liberation (9,12b), a definitive pardon (10,11–18). If Jesus' life at the Father's side is the source of our salvation, it must be added that this eternal life continues and encompasses his act of dying on the cross. The gospel writers showed the Risen Lord with his wounds still visible. John used the verb "to be lifted up" to refer both to Jesus' death and his glorification. Hebrews expresses the same thing by the image of Christ, the high priest, entering heaven "with his own blood" (9,12).

At the end of the liturgy, it was the custom for the high priest to go out to the Temple court to bless the faithful who were waiting there. This aspect as well is present in Christ's pilgrimage:

So Christ, too, after having been offered up once and for all in order to take away the sins of many, will appear a second time, not to bear sin, but for the salvation of those waiting for him. (9,28)

To sum up: the epistle to the Hebrews describes the way of Jesus, particularly his Passover from death to life, as a cosmic liturgy of forgiveness, of reconciliation. In celebrating the Yom Kippur liturgy, the high priest traced out a path in the Temple, a path that symbolically linked the people and God. According to Hebrews, Christ traced out a similar path; he opened the true Way between earth and heaven. Before his coming, the way to the sanctuary, that is, to God, was not yet manifest (9,8). Now, however, we are sure of possessing "an access road (*eisodos*) to the sanctuary by the blood of Jesus, a brand-new and living road which he inaugurated for us through the curtain" (10,19–20). The word *eisodos* "evokes those boulevards or avenues that led up to the Greek and Egyptian sanctuaries, and where processions were held."[5] But this Road is alive; it is the incarnate Son of God (cf. John 14,6). As a result of the earthly existence of the Son, as a result of his "flesh" (cf. John 1,14), we know the Father, and henceforth we can live in full communion with him.

Christ's pilgrimage is thus the source of joyful confidence (10,19 *parrhēsia*) for us. It provides us, moreover, with a firm hope. Hebrews speaks of this hope in verses that link admirably the way of Christ and the Christian life:

> ... that we may be strongly encouraged to take hold of the hope that is set before us. In it, we have a kind of anchor for our soul, strong and fast. It goes in behind the curtain, where Jesus, as a forerunner, went in for us, when he became a high priest for ever according to the order of Melchizedek. (6,18b-20)

These verses sum up the epistle's understanding of Christ's role in God's plan. Having become one of us, or better yet, the one who represents us all, the Son entered, as a human being, into everlasting life, into a full communion with the Father. In consequence, it is as if a part of ourselves, the most important part, were already on the other side. Jesus is our *prodromos*, our precursor or forerunner:

> In ordinary usage, *prodromos* was used for the first fruits and vegetables to ripen, for emissaries, for more rapid runners who passed all their competitors; for the vanguard that explored the terrain before the arrival of the army, for the quick ship sent before the fleet of cargo ships to guide them; it was the first to come into port and, in case of a storm, it was the one that had to look for a secure berth. The metaphor thus goes together well with that of the anchor (v. 19) ... The religious nuance is assured by the fact that the *dromos* or "way of God" was also the sacred way, a wide paved avenue leading up to the Temple ... In any event, "the gap must not be too wide between the forerunner and those who follow him, otherwise he would not be their forerunner. The forerunner and the followers are necessarily on the same road; the former leads the way, the others close in on him" (Chrysostom).[6]

That is our hope, based not on a mere dream or wish but on the road already followed by Christ, our high priest who is alive for ever, the one who goes before us and who shows us the way (cf. 2,10) through the "curtain," the wall that separates us from God.

A *pilgrim people*

The epistle to the Hebrews thus follows the same movement that we have already discerned in the rest of the New Testament: in and through Christ, the way of God becomes the way of humanity. By looking now at the manner in which the author implicitly describes those to whom he is addressing himself, we will arrive at the same result from an entirely different angle.

First of all, Hebrews never speaks to individuals but always to the community of believers. Faithful to the teaching of the Scriptures, for the author God's partner is always *the people of God* as a whole. This continuity with the Hebrew tradition is reinforced by an expression commonly used in the epistle to describe the faithful: they are "the heirs of the promise" (6,17; cf. 9,15; 6,12).[7] That explains their link with Abraham (6,13–15; 11,8–9) as well as with all the important actors in the history of salvation (ch. 11). In Hebrews, "the promise" and "the inheritance" are synonyms for *salvation* (1,14; cf. 2,3; 5,9; 9,28b) and very close, in the semantic field of the epistle, to *hope* (6,18; 7,19): a reality that is both present (6,4) and future, linked to a call (9,15; cf. 3,1) and implying, as for Abraham (11,8f), the need to leave everything behind in order to be a pilgrim with God. Like the patriarchs, in this world Christians are "refugees" who must "take hold of the hope set before them" (6,18; cf. 13,14).

And so, for Hebrews the community of believers is God's people *on the move*. Being Christian, of course, means already being an intimate (*metochos*) of Christ (3,14), a sharer (*metochos*) in the Holy Spirit (6,4); it means having already "tasted the heavenly gift ... and the powers of the age to come" (6,4–5). And yet, at present, believers are still undergoing a process of growth (5,11ff); they are confronted with trials (2,18) and can fall along the way. In this sense, the experience of the Israelites led by Moses in the wilderness is still relevant for them. The author of Hebrews reflects at great length on Psalm 95 (3,7—4,11). This psalm describes "the day of trial" in the wilderness, when the people hardened their hearts and lacked trust in God (PGod 38–40). The Lord declared that these disobedient people would never enter his rest and warns future generations not to behave in the same way.

Hebrews recalls this warning, and applies it to the situation of Christians. They should remain firm in faith to the end (3,14) and not lag behind (4,1). For God has established a new "today" for us (4,7), a sabbath day of rest (4,9). Entering the Promised Land under Joshua was only a figure of the true rest still waiting for God's people (4,8–9). This day of rest still lies ahead of us; it is coming closer (10,25). Christ has already fully entered it (4,10; cf. 9,24; 10,11–13), and by our fidelity we will enter as well (4,3.11).

The theology of the sabbath found in Hebrews enables a whole other dimension of the faith of Israel to be integrated into the Christian pilgrimage. The true Sabbath, the definitive time of repose prepared by God since the foundation of the world (4,3–4), is neither the entrance into Canaan nor the seventh day of the week: it is the Day of the Lord, the goal of our pilgrimage, the entrance into full intimacy with God. Christ entered this rest by his own pilgrimage, by his Passover. In this respect, it is interesting to note that the feast of Yom Kippur is traditionally a day of complete fasting and rest (Lev 23,26–32). In Judaism it is called "the Day" and also "the Sabbath of sabbaths."[8] When Hebrews describes the way of Christ as a cosmic liturgy of reconciliation, then, it is a way of saying that in his company we enter the true Sabbath, the day of a perfect communion between God and humanity. All at once certain things Jesus did, notably his acts of healing on the sabbath day, take on a whole new significance. As the true Lord of the sabbath, Jesus does not violate or neglect the Torah in any way; he gives it its full meaning.

Finally, for Hebrews the community of believers, God's pilgrim people, is a *community of worship*. Like Israel in the desert, the faithful make up a *qahal*, an *ekklēsia*, an assembly called together by the Lord to enter into relationship with him. We have already insisted at length on the liturgical dimension of this epistle. If Jesus is our high priest, then we are his congregation. By his gift of self, by his sacrifice, he has made us holy (10,10; cf. 2,11) and perfect (10,14). The word translated by "to make perfect," incidentally, was used for ordination to the priesthood (cf. 5,9).[9] We are henceforth a holy people (cf. 6,10), a people of priests qualified to offer authentic worship to the living God (9,14; cf. 12,28), a sacrifice of praise and sharing (13,15–16). Because of Christ, we can "approach with confidence the throne of grace, in order to obtain mercy and to find grace" (4,16). The verb translated "to approach" is likewise part of the vocabulary of the cult; our pilgrimage is thus also a liturgical procession (cf. 7,19.25; 10,1.22; 11,6).

And here, another parallel intervenes. Just as Christ accomplishes the liturgy of reconciliation of which Yom Kippur was a preliminary sketch, so does the Christian *ekklēsia* re-live, on a different level, the ratification of the covenant on Sinai:

> You did not approach something palpable: blazing fire and darkness and gloom and storm and trumpet blast and words so loud that those who heard them begged that no further message be given to them ... But you approached Mount Zion and the city of the living God, the heavenly Jerusalem, and myriads of angels in festal gathering, and the assembly of the firstborn whose names are written in heaven, and God the judge of all, and spirits of the righteous who have been perfected, and Jesus the mediator of a new covenant, and atoning blood more eloquent than that of Abel. (12,18–24)

Likewise, Hebrews contrasts "the blood of goats and calves" used by Moses to ratify the Sinai covenant (9,12ff) with the sacrifice of Christ, the only truly efficacious one. In both cases, there is a progression from a material and earthly reality to a spiritual and heavenly one, from a symbol to its true meaning. This shift of levels, however, occurs in the context of a broader continuity. Christians are longing for the "city to come" (13,14). The Hebrew patriarchs, for their part, were looking for this same heavenly home (11,13–16), and Moses himself behaved like someone who sees the Invisible (11,27). The principle of this continuity is *faith*, "the present reality of things hoped for, the proof of what we cannot see" (11,1). To believe is to live here and now in the light of a future beyond all our imaginings; it is to translate into the daily events of a seemingly ordinary existence something of the world of the invisible, of the reality of the living God. It means, in short, becoming a pilgrim of the absolute, with no permanent attachments in this world.

This notion of Christians as pilgrims is a major theme of another New Testament writing, the first letter of PETER. The apostle exhorts the faithful "as foreigners (*paroikoi*) and sojourners (*parepidēmoi*)" (1 Peter 2,11) spread across the world (1,1).[10] They are not at home on this earth: their existence is a sojourn (*paroikia*) in a foreign land (1,17). In this respect it is interesting to

175

note that our word "parish" comes from the same root. By its etymology it signifies the dwelling of those who are on a journey, the home of women and men who have not definitively settled down in the places where they live.

The first letter of Peter is addressed to Christians who have come for the most part from paganism. In the old days, writes the author, you followed your passions blindly (1,14; 4,3f); your life-style led nowhere (1,18); you were "like sheep going astray" (2,25). But now, on account of the resurrection of Christ, you have been "brought to new birth in a living hope" (1,3) by an incorruptible seed—the Word of God (1,23), the Gospel (1,25).

Like newborn babies (2,2), those who were baptized have entered a new life. From now on they walk in the footsteps of Christ (2,21; cf. 3,18). They have become a holy people, the house of God built of living stones (2,4–10). They are a community whose life is based on love (1,22; 3,8; 4,8) and that even consents to suffer for the name of Christ (4,12–19), thus imitating his behavior (2,19–24). The way Christians live should be a sign for those who have not yet embraced the faith, so that they too may discover and give glory to the one true God (2,12–15; 3,1.16).

In the letter to the Ephesians, the author had written to the Gentiles who became Christians that they were no longer strangers and foreigners (*xenoi kai paroikoi*) but fellow citizens of the saints and members of the household of God (Eph 2,19). Peter likewise stresses the fact that the former pagans are now members of the family (2,5; 4,17), but for him that does not imply that they have ceased to be pilgrims. On the contrary, by their baptism they have broken their ties with a world doomed to disappear (cf. 4,7). They have entered on the way of the Lord traced out in the midst of human history, like a path of light, by the Passover of Jesus Christ.

A spirituality for the road

The epistle to the Hebrews describes the Christian community as a people of pilgrims following the way of Christ, our guide (Heb 2,10; 12,2) and our shepherd (13,20). A whole spirituality follows from this deeply biblical conception of the life of faith. That seems even to have been the reason the epistle was com-

176

posed: to encourage the faithful to remain on this road and to keep going forward. This purpose lies behind the advice given concerning Christian behavior—the good habits to be encouraged and the faults to be criticized. It is the foundation of the rule of life for believers.

If the Christian life is a pilgrimage, then the only real misfortune is to turn off the road, to fall away in the middle of the journey. For Hebrews that is the basic sin,[11] the thing to be avoided at all costs. To describe this eventuality in a precise manner, the epistle employs the verb *pararreo* (2,1), often used to speak of boats and meaning "to slip away, to be washed away or to drift away." The image is one of leaving the route laid out and of going astray. The prefix *"para-,"* incidentally, which can be used in Greek to signify "beside," provides several expressions for the vocabulary of sin in Hebrews: *parabasis* (overstepping, transgression: 2,2; 9,15), *paraiteomai* (to reject, avoid; to beg: 12,19.25), *parakoē* (unwillingness to hear; disobedience: 2,2), *parapiptō* (to fall beside, outside; to go astray, miss; to fall away: 6,6), *parapheromai* (to be carried off, away; to be led away: 13,9). To sin is to leave the path, to "miss the boat." It is also to wander around, to be deluded, to go astray (*planaō:* 3,10; 5,2); to withdraw, to draw back (*hypostellomai:* 10,38.39); to turn away, to reject (*apostrephomai:* 12,25); to leave behind, to desert the others (*engkataleipō:* 10,25); to fall short, to fail to reach, to exclude oneself from God's grace (*hystereō:* 4,1; 12,15). And from his commentary on Psalm 95 our author draws another image: the opposite of a life with God is the hardening of one's heart (3,8.13), the refusal to listen "today" to God's voice and to follow it (cf. 12,25). Two synonyms describe perfectly those who leave the road in this way to settle down into a self-centered existence: *apistia* (3,12.19) and *apeitheia* (4,6.11), a lack of trust.

The life of faith, on the other hand, involves constant progress, perpetual growth; there is no room at all for turning back (6,4ff). Hebrews has a beautiful word to describe the essential nature of this life, *parrhēsia*, usually translated by "assurance" or "confidence," although these words give only a faint echo of its rich significance. *Parrhēsia* is the attitude of joyful confidence, of trust-filled, almost carefree freedom, found in the person who knows he or she is loved and accepted and who thus feels fully at home, like a child who runs from room to room of a large country house where he has always spent his holidays. The word evokes the same attitude expressed by Jesus when he used the word "Abba": confident trust rooted in love, a source of energy to go forward. Those who live in this manner know they have no need to defend or justify themselves or to prove anything to anybody, and so they are free to become more and more deeply what they are in their heart of hearts.

Because of Christ's coming and the gift of his life, we have this *parrhēsia* by which we enter into full communion with God (10,19) and come closer to him (4,16). And yet this attitude, a consequence of faith, has nothing automatic about it; it can be lost. That is why the epistle to the Hebrews constantly exhorts believers to cling to it. "Do not lose your *parrhēsia*" (10,35). We are God's household, "as long as we hold on to our *parrhēsia* and the *kauchēma* of hope" (3,6). The word *kauchēma*, often translated by "boasting," has a meaning very close to *parrhēsia*. It refers to what we can boast of, in other words the source of our joy and our confidence. Hebrews encourages the faithful to remain close to this source and to drink from it often, in order to keep alive our identity as Christians.

It is in this sense that, for Hebrews, faith is practically a synonym for fidelity. To be fully itself, it cannot simply be reduced to "peak experiences" or kindle short-lived fireworks; it must become incarnate in the warp and woof of daily existence. In the life of a pilgrim, much importance is placed upon *perseverance* (*makrothumia*) and *endurance* (*hypomonē*). We must cling to the faith that we confess (4,14; cf. 12,28). As was the case for Abraham and the other believers of past ages, only those who persevere to the end will inherit the promised salvation (6,12–15). We are in need of endurance (10,36), especially when trials arise (12,7), for if we remain faithful these difficulties will transform us, making us resemble the Son more closely (12,5–13). Christ, in fact, went through the trial in his own life, in order to express in a human existence the unfathomable depths of the divine mercy (2,17–18; 4,15; 5,7–9).

How can we be faithful to the very end? Hebrews gives an answer to this question: by going back to the beginning. "Remember the first days" (10,32); "[we must] hold firmly to the end the confidence we had at the beginning" (3,14). It is a matter of going back to the roots again and again, to that initial encounter with God when all we needed was given. This movement is in no way a regression, a turning back, for the gift we received at the beginning was a gift of hope (6,18), a hope that must grow and blossom until the end (6,11; cf. 10,23). Paying attention to the others who are walking on the same road is another support for our perseverance: "let us keep our eyes on one another so as to incite each other to love and to do good works . . . [let us be] imitators of those who, by their faith and perseverance, inherit the things promised" (10,24; 6,12b). The simple fact of knowing that we are not alone, that others (and above all Christ himself), have undergone and are still undergoing the same difficulties and temptations and yet remain faithful, gives courage to confront the combat of the spiritual life (cf. 12,3–4). But in the final analysis, the true source of a Christian's perseverance is God's own faithfulness (10,23). Living by faith (cf.10,38) means acting on the basis of this faithfulness; it means believing in the One-who-comes and taking his promises seriously. Faith makes the future present and enables us to see the Invisible (cf. 11,1).

The author of Hebrews sums up admirably his vision of the Christian life by taking up the Pauline image of the race. In this book, however, it is above all an endurance test, a kind of marathon. What enables the believer to persevere is the presence of the community of believers across the centuries and, above all, a relationship with Jesus Christ, who already covered the course and who is our companion as we run. This image allows the author to link up human effort and God's activity in Christ, personal responsibility and the presence of others, faith as a journey and sin as that which holds us back and makes us stumble:

> We too, therefore, since we have such a cloud of witnesses all around us, let us throw off all that weighs us down and the sin that clings round us, and let us run with perseverance the contest proposed to us, keeping our eyes fixed on Jesus, the model of faith from beginning to end. Instead of the joy that was his for the taking, he endured a cross, scorning its shame, and then took his seat at the right of God's throne. Reflect on the one who put up with such a contradiction against himself at the hands of sinners, so that you will not lose heart and grow weary. (12,1–3)

Questions for Reflection

1. How does the figure of Melchizedek (Gen 14; Ps 110; Heb 7) help us better to understand Jesus and his mission?

2. Hebrews uses the term "sacrifice" (Heb 10,12) to describe Christ's gift of his life in order to bring us forgiveness. How does this help us to understand the true meaning of sacrifice? As disciples of Christ, what is the "sacrifice" we offer (see also Rom 12,1–2; Heb 13,15–16)?

3. The epistle to the Hebrews develops a whole theology of the sabbath (Heb 3,7—4,11). Where do we see the seeds of this theology in the earthly life of Jesus as told in the gospels?

4. Should we live today as "foreigners and sojourners" (1 Peter 2,11), as pilgrims in this world? Why? How?

5. Hebrews employs the words "assurance, confidence" (*parrhēsia*: Heb 3,6; 4,16; 10,19.35), "perseverance" (*makrothumia*: 6,12.15), and "endurance" (*hypomonē*: 10,36; 12,1; cf. 12,7) to describe some basic attitudes of the Christian life. What significance do these words have for our pilgrimage of faith? What other words could we use to translate these values, to make them more understandable to people today?

Notes

[1] C. Spicq, O.P., *L'Epître aux Hébreux* (Paris: Gabalda, 1977), p. 56.
[2] As is clear from the rest of this chapter, Hebrews uses other Scriptural images and comparisons to describe the career of Jesus: Moses and the establishment of the covenant on Sinai, Melchisedek and Psalm 110, etc. But the image of the high priest celebrating the Yom Kippur liturgy seems to be the dominant metaphor.
[3] Spicq, pp. 152–153.
[4] Cf. 10,5ff where, by applying to Christ Psalm 40 quoted from the Greek Bible, the author contrasts the sacrifices of the old economy with the body of Christ formed by God. And in 2 Cor 5, 1ff. the notions of "body," "heaven" and "not made by hand" are all associated. In any event, by using the expression *ou cheiropoiētos*, "not made-by-hand," the author links up with one constant tendency in the faith of Israel, that of not fixing the pilgrim God to a particular place (cf. Acts 7,47–50; 17,24). If the "better tent" here is in fact the body of Christ, then Hebrews goes even further, not merely situating God beyond everything finite, but seeing this "beyond" as incarnate at the heart of human history by the pilgrimage of the Son, the meeting-place between

humanity and its Creator. The age-old opposition between transcendence and imminence is thus finally overcome.

[5]Spicq, p. 170.

[6]Spicq, p. 116.

[7]Ernst Käsemann, *The Wandering People of God: An Investigation of the Letter to the Hebrews* (2nd ed. 1957; Minneapolis: Augsburg Publ. House, 1984),pp. 26–35, analyzes the vocabulary of the promise in Hebrews. For him, the notion of the "wandering people of God" is a key for the interpretation of the epistle. Unfortunately this work, which contains many original and valuable intuitions, leans too heavily on the thesis that Hebrews borrowed a Gnostic schema to be completely convincing. Could not Gnostic circles have equally well adapted to their own needs elements of Christian doctrine? A recent American commentary likewise uses the theme of pilgrimage as a basis for understanding Hebrews: Robert Jewett, *Letter to Pilgrims: A Commentary on the Epistle to the Hebrews* (New York: The Pilgrim Press, 1981).

[8]Joseph Kalir, *Introduction to Judaism* (Washington DC: University Press of America, 1980), pp. 15–17.

[9]*Traduction Oecuménique de la Bible* (TOB), note *h* on Hebrews 5,9, p. 680.

[10]The two words *paroikoi* and *parepidēmoi* were both terms used in ancient times to refer to people who were not in their own land, who were not citizens of the place in which they happened to be, with all the rights which that entailed. More exactly, the *paroikoi* were foreigners who were residing for a period of time in a country; although they were not citizens, they usually had certain rights that were legally recognized. The *parepidēmoi*, a less common expression, referred to travellers who were just passing through. See John H. Elliott, *A Home for the Homeless: A Sociological Exegesis of I Peter, Its Situation and Strategy* (Philadelphia: Fortress Press, 1981), pp. 21–58. This author views 1 Peter as addressed not merely to foreigners and sojourners in a metaphorical sense but to actual foreigners, displaced persons who accepted the Gospel. He sees the purpose of the letter as that of convincing them that their situation was not a deplorable one, but one that could help them better to understand the faith they were professing. Although sociologically speaking they were homeless, or even outcasts, in fact they were "of the household of God" (1 Peter 2,5; 4,17). For the terminology of "foreigners and sojourners" see also C. Spicq, O.P., *Vie chrétienne et pérégrination selon le Nouveau Testament* (Paris: Cerf, 1972), pp. 59–76.

[11]Käsemann, pp. 45–48, remarks that Hebrews is interested not in sin in general, still less in "original sin," but only in the sin of persons already baptized, those already walking along the way of the Lord.

EIGHT

The Drama of
Revelation

At this point in our journey, it may be useful to orient ourselves by taking up again, from another point of view, the notion of faith as a pilgrimage, as the "way of the Lord" to be followed, and the role of the Scriptures as the motivation for this vision.

Let us begin simply with ourselves as human beings, as we enter the world, with no preconceptions or preconditions.

At birth, we are set almost entirely under the sign of potentiality. A host of possibilities lie before us; we are heirs to a material and spiritual universe of apparently unlimited dimensions. In this respect, even someone with no explicit faith who reflects on the marvel that is a human being can hardly fail to understand the words of the psalmist: "You have made him little less than a god, you have crowned him with glory and beauty, made him lord of the works of your hands, put all things under his feet" (Ps 8,5–6 NJB).

It is precisely this range of possibilities offered to us that is the other side of our open, incomplete character. In fact, compared to human beings, other creatures are already born in a more "finished" state. Baby birds or puppies very quickly learn how to put to use all their powers. Human children, by comparison, develop more slowly. They are more helpless, more vulnerable; it takes them long years to reach maturity. It can even be said that the higher the field of our activity, the longer the period of apprenticeship needed. With respect to the spiritual life, the summit of human existence, can it ever be said that we have fully arrived?

Our eminent dignity as human beings is thus inseparably linked to our incompleteness, to our basic vulnerability. But we are not only born incomplete; we carry within ourselves a will to grow, to realize our potentialities, to widen our universe in all its dimensions. By our very makeup, we are beings of desire, and this means beings with a history, beings on the road. Our life consists of a progressive growth in awareness of all that is in us and around us, through a constant interchange with our environment. Slowly, starting from our innate gifts and a two-way relationship with our material and human milieu, our identity is forged; we become a person related to other persons, a microcosm of the universe.

At the same time, we must immediately add that, in itself, the dynamic makeup of the human being remains ambiguous. Our road is not a simple path upward towards the light. This ambiguity makes itself felt in different ways, and gives human life its specifically moral—and sometimes tragic—dimension.

On the one hand, the process of development has nothing automatic about it. It works through the intelligence and the will of the subject. It involves a whole series of explicit or implicit choices, and each choice determines in part those that follow. What we do today makes tomorrow's tasks either easier or more difficult, by pointing us in one direction or another. And it is quite possible to make mistakes: blinded by its superficial glitter, its apparent plausibility, we may be seduced into choosing the easy way out, the path that leads not to a broadening of horizons but to a shrinking of them, to a cut-rate, and ultimately illusory, contentment.

Moreover, the shrinking of horizons is not always the result of an intellectual error. It can also arise from a lack of moral courage. Leaving the tried-and-true for a world still unknown is never an easy decision. Setting out on a journey always involves a risk and, each time life offers us an opportunity to know it more deeply, fear can win out over the desire to discover more about the universe in which we live and to take our place in it appropriately. As a result, the growth of a human being often resembles more closely a—sometimes bitter—struggle against inner and outer resistances than a predictable and painless blossoming of our talents.

The environment in which we live likewise reinforces the ambiguous character of human dynamism. Human society takes shape out of innumerable personal decisions which go far back in time and which accumulate like a sediment, a layer of soil on our present landscape. Every civilization has its particular customs and habits, its cherished notions, its own values that either foster or inhibit the development of the whole human being. Whether we happen to like it or not, interdependence is a rule of life on this planet. Those who have the misfortune to be born in a context particularly resistant to an increase of light will find it still more difficult to make the choices that will allow their freedom to grow and to develop correctly. In this respect, the warning that the sins of the parents will fall upon the children, the grandchildren and the great-grandchildren remains permanently relevant.

To sum up, the makeup of the human being, our incomparable dignity, can be expressed by the fact that we are not born ready-made; we are beings-on-the-move who have to collaborate in our own creation. In us and around us, we have all we need to attain our full humanity; we have, in addition, the desire to do so. Nevertheless, in all this there is nothing automatic. Instead of dealing with the reality of the world and of ourselves, we can decide to close our eyes, or more probably keep them half-shut. We can allow the force of our desire to become weakened by the search for counterfeits and subterfuges. We can prefer our own comfort, or the approval of others, to the arduous apprenticeship of reality. We can, finally, simply be mistaken or disoriented: after all, how is it possible to find a way in the midst of the influences that assail us on all sides? How can we make authentic choices? Does reality even exist, or are we, when all is said and done, merely prisoners of appearances and opinions?

The most encompassing context of all

If this is the human condition, it is evident that it includes both grandeur and tragedy; it is an invitation to go further and a riddle to be solved. One of the great merits of what is known as religion has always been to sense that this riddle cannot be definitively solved by remaining on a purely human level: Reality itself, absolute Reality, must reveal its secret. The paradox proclaimed by religion is that, left to ourselves, we will never reach the fulfillment we long for; we can only become fully ourselves by entering into a relationship with a higher order of being. At the same time, it is obvious that this higher order, this ultimate Reality, and its consequences for human life, can be— and has been—envisaged in a great many ways. The most cruel irony of all would be for religion, in the name of the ostensible rights of the divine, to frustrate the natural dynamism of human beings, their aspiration to the fullness of being, their thirst for happiness. Cannot one expression of the tragedy of the Western world be found in the fact that some have believed that, in order for humanity to grow and reach maturity, it was necessary to proclaim the death of God, viewed implicitly as a tyrannical patriarch jealous of the liberty of his children? And has not an even more serious tragedy followed from this: where it did in fact come about, the death of the father did not lead to the best of all possible worlds for the children but rather to a loss of historical continuity, a slow evaporation of true hope and an evisceration of the depths of existence—in short, to the death of the human soul.

Let us beware, however, of identifying the great Judeo-Christian tradition with its counterfeits. In these chapters, and in a preceding work, we have attempted to discover how the message of the Hebrew and the Christian Scriptures responds to the exegencies of the human spirit and points it toward fulfillment. Far from impeding the dynamism of life, the Bible describes for us the way of God himself, the pilgrim God. And so, if humans are beings on the move, precisely in this they resemble their Creator more closely. The Hebrew Scriptures reveal the way of the Lord through the existence of a people: gradually, in the course of human history, God's face becomes more discernible and the human journey receives an orientation and a guarantee. The call of the pilgrim God sets us on the only road that will not sooner or later be mired in isolation and insignificance. As a result, authentic life can be seen as the imitation of God, as the attempt to walk in his footsteps.

In the period that preceded the New Testament, the way of the Lord was something that had to be discerned. Its raw material was found in the events of the life of the people of Israel; it was transmitted in story form, systematized into a teaching, the Torah—but it only appeared fleetingly on the surface of history. In Jesus Christ, however, the way of the Lord took human shape, and became identified with the life of a particular human being. All at once imitation is a real possibility; God's footsteps have become fully accessible, and we can place our own feet in them. Still more, by the resurrection of Christ and the gift of his Spirit, the way of the Lord comes to humanity not from without but from within. The ancient prophecy of a new covenant, of a Torah written on people's hearts, becomes a reality, and God's pilgrimage in this world takes shape in the existence of a community with a universal outlook. In this respect, the Christian Church represents the culmination of God's plan: the Body of Christ, it is the place where the Mystery of God weds itself definitively to our human reality. As a consequence, it widens to the fullest possible extent the horizons of being, and offers an authentic context for the full development of the human person.

When the Church turns to its sacred books in order to come closer to its roots, it rediscovers its identity as a people on the road. It sees itself as a community that lives out in the present the paschal pilgrimage of its founder and, in this way, translates the way of the Lord into the concrete conditions of human history. The Church does not, of course, represent the culmination of God's plan insofar as it is an immobile and self-sufficient institution concerned only about its own survival, but rather when it witnesses to Christ and his Kingdom, when it is a sign held up before all humanity of divine love made flesh. In other words, the Church becomes fully herself, the "city to come" (Heb 13,14), the "new Jerusalem" (Rev 21) that breaks into our present day, when she lives deeply her calling to be a people of pilgrims.

The Bible does not give us ready-made answers to our questions about the meaning and the problems of existence. But it situates our life, with all its limits and its impossibilities, in the widest, the most encompassing context possible. At the beginning of this chapter we described human existence as a permanent attempt to actualize one's potentialities, to widen one's universe. At the same time, we noted the difficulties of this enterprise. In this respect, the Bible presents us with the ultimate horizon of our activity; the way of the Lord that it traces out shows us the definitive contours of our existence. And it does this without limiting our freedom or determining it in advance, because the way it offers is not a list of duties or a program to be put into practice but a Life that one enters, a Life of communion.

To put it another way, when we meditate on the Scriptures we are invited to take our place in a great epic, a drama that began the day an unknown God encountered Abraham on his journey and invited that man to accompany him to the land of the promise. The art of a dramatist channels the energies and talents of actors without taking away their creativity; it gives meaning to their contribution by situating it in a wider framework. Faith orients and gives meaning to our life in a similar fashion. It does not do away with our human gifts but places them in a universal context.

This means among other things that believers are not limited by the values and customs of their own society. In their relationship with their God, they benefit from thousands of years of human experience. Their task, and it is a difficult one, is to manage to integrate the particular needs of their own time and the great Judeo-Christian tradition handed down to them. In addition, believers are not required to count only upon their own forces. On the one hand, they receive the support of a community of faith, and on the other, they know that the Holy Spirit, God's own energy, undergirds and guides their efforts. And in contrast to a play or a film, the believer's role is not written out ahead of time in a script. Each person has to work out this role day after day under the guidance of the Holy Spirit, by means of prayer, listening to the Word and membership in a community of faith. The Judeo-Christian pilgrimage thus possesses an even more dramatic character than the work of human authors. Its principal lines have been laid out, notably by the Passover of Jesus Christ; its happy ending is assured by the Good News of the resurrection; but within this framework everything has to be invented, through a confrontation with the exigencies of life, in each new day given by God.

Of all the books of the New Testament, it is the last one that undoubtedly helps us understand best the dramatic character of biblical revelation. Instead of making use of the description of past events or the pragmatic language of exhortation, the author of the Book of REVELATION, also known as the Apocalypse of John, translates the pilgrimage of faith into powerful, unforgettable and often enigmatic images. In this way he helps us see, beneath the surface of events, the true significance of salvation history; he reveals the drama of creation in all its depth and breadth.

The Book of Revelation has often been read as a more or less literal description of an impending future, of the coming "end of the world." In fact, rather than attempting to describe future events, the work wants to reveal to us the *depths* of history, to uncover its ultimate and transhistoric meaning. That is why the images and symbols of this book have been applied more or less successfully to the most diverse historical events. Rather than taking this diversity as an indication of the author's mental confusion, should we not see it as a proof of his perception of the unity of God's plan through all the successive phases?

A complete investigation of Revelation does not enter into the scope of this book.[1] We shall limit ourselves to indicating the general structure of the work and choose, as examples, several images that confirm the discoveries we have already made on our pilgrimage through the books of the New Testament.

The basic framework of the Book of Revelation is formed by four series of seven symbolic realities: seven letters, seven seals, seven trumpets, and seven cups or bowls. The four narrative sections thus formed trace out, with growing precision, the progressive revelation of God's designs. The relationship between the four septenaries is not of a chronological order, that is, they do not succeed one another in time. It is rather something similar to the prologue of John's gospel (John 1,1–18): a movement from relative indetermination, from a more global perspective, to a greater precision, something like a camera lens or a telescope that is gradually brought into sharper focus.[2]

The four symbols—dictating letters, opening a sealed scroll, sounding trumpets, pouring out the contents of bowls—all describe the transmission of something, with perhaps a note of ever increasing urgency. The first three symbols all clearly have to do with the communication of a message, but here too there is a sense of greater and greater immediacy. First of all, letters are written to criticize and to encourage "the seven Churches," a symbol of the totality of God's people. Then, when the seals of the book are broken open, this act is immediately translated into events of the history of salvation described symbolically. Next, the act of sounding a trumpet indicates the announcement of something imminent of great importance. Finally, with the last image the intellectual aspect disappears completely and we are confronted with the naked reality: the biblical image of the cup links admirably the two sides of divine judgment—trial and blessing.[3]

As the drama of Revelation works itself out, the recipients of "the revelation of Jesus Christ" (Rev 1,1) are thus involved in an ever more intimate fashion. "The mystery of God" (10,7) descends to earth from heaven; it leaves the letters and the book in order to encounter us personally. Or, to invert the image, the experience resembles that of reading a good suspense novel or watching a successful play: at a given moment, all distance is abolished and we enter fully into what up to then was only words on a page or actors on a stage. With the significant difference, however, that here we are not dealing with a psychological effect created by the art of a novelist or playwright but a true, objective movement, the result of God's activity. God comes toward humanity; little by little, the way of the Lord becomes our own. The day comes when we become aware of our role in God's story and begin to live it out consciously. In fact, there is no better illustration of the creative art of a dramatist than the activity of God. Starting from nothing, God creates free persons with which he populates his work, a work which is nothing other than his own life, the road along which he walks.

The experience of the reader of the Book of Revelation thus reflects the whole course of salvation history, the same reality that John's gospel describes as the movement from "the Law" to "grace and truth" (John 1,17), and Saint Paul as that from "the letter" to "the Spirit" (2 Cor 3,6ff). For the Book of Revelation just as for the entire New Testament, what makes this movement possible is the coming of Jesus Christ among us, and notably his Passover through death to life in all its fullness.

190

Once again, the relationship between the four narrative sections of this book is not chronological, but rather one of a growing precision and realization of the way of the Lord. The first septenary, that of the letters (Rev 1,9—3,22), provides us with a global, indeterminate overview of divine revelation. At the center is the vision of Daniel's Son of Man (Dan 7,13–14) walking among the seven golden lampstands that represent the seven Churches while holding in his hand the seven stars, an image of the angels responsible for the Churches (Rev 1,9–20). This majestic and terrifying being has divine features but is immediately identified, albeit still in an allusive way, with Jesus Christ:

"I am the First and the Last, and the Living One; I was dead, and now I am alive for ever and ever; I possess the keys of death and of Hades." (1,17b-18)

The Son of Man dictates seven letters to John, one for each of the angels in charge of the seven Churches. The letters are all similar in structure: they identify the heavenly author, praise or blame the readers and then exhort them, and finally mention certain promises and encourage them to "listen to what the Spirit is saying to the Churches." Here we have, in a nutshell, all the essential elements of Holy Scripture.

The seven letters dictated by the Son of Man are explicitly addressed to communities known to the author of Revelation in seven cities of the Roman province of Asia (our Asia Minor). But they include a great many allusions to the Hebrew Scriptures that deal with all the periods of bible history. Moreover, if we recall that, in the Bible, the number seven usually stands for the earthly totality of something, it is not hard to see these chapters as a global, allegorical presentation of divine revelation as a whole. In that case, the important thing in the entire scene is the identification of the principal author of revelation. Behind the sacred texts ("the letters"), behind their inspired human author ("John"), behind even the powers that inhabit the universe and direct the course of history ("the angels"), we glimpse the figure of the Son of Man "walking among the seven golden lampstands" (2,1). In the final analysis, he is the one who reveals, by his Spirit, God's intentions to redeemed humanity, and he is also the one who brings about what he has promised. John presents him implicitly as the principal actor who presides over all of salvation history.

The second septenary, that of the seven seals (4,1—8,1), takes up this same idea in another form. Instead of the letters, there is a scroll or book that is sealed shut. We can interpret this symbol on different levels: it is "the book of life" that reveals the definitive fate of each person (cf. 13,8; 20,12), the divine plan that is worked out in stages in the history of the universe, and finally the biblical books that communicate to us an ever clearer view of this plan.

Following an introductory scene where we see the Creator surrounded by his heavenly court (ch. 4), John glimpses the "scroll . . . sealed with seven seals" in God's hand (5,1). At first it seems that "no one was able . . . to open the book and read it" (5,3). But the seer's sadness soon receives consolation as the heavenly liturgy continues. "A Lamb standing, as if slain" appears in the middle of the throne, and we learn that he is

> worthy to take the scroll
> and to open the seals,
> for [he] was slain and purchased for God,
> with [his] blood,
> persons of every race and language and people and nation;
> [he] made them, for our God,
> a kingdom of priests ruling over the earth. (5,9–10)

Then the Lamb opens the seven seals, one after another, and each time something dramatic happens. We witness a symbolic presentation of the history of the human race. Although it begins well (6,1–2), quite soon it falls prey to the forces of discord and violence (6,3–8). Some, however, are saved from the powers of evil: first twelve thousand persons from each of the tribes of Israel (7,1–8) and then "a great crowd, which no one could count" (7,9), that the Lamb "would shepherd and lead the way to springs of living water" (7,17).

The second part of the book thus arrives at a result identical to the first. At the center of history is the figure of the dead and risen Christ. He is the one who has the keys that make it possible for us to understand fully the way of the Lord. Or, to put it another way, all of human history is nothing other than a progressive revelation of his identity (cf. 1,1). Beyond this common structure, however, there is an evolution in the direction of greater precision. The glorious Son of Man is replaced by the "Lamb standing, as if slain" (5,6), an image that is clearly more incarnate, where the mystery of Jesus' saving death is referred to by allusions to the paschal lamb (Ex 12) and indirectly to the Servant of Second Isaiah (Isa 53,7). And whereas the Son of Man is simply *walking* in the midst of the Churches (Rev 2,1), the Lamb *will shepherd* the faithful and *lead the way* to springs of living water (7,17). The way of God revealed by Jesus Christ becomes the way of Christians, the road of the Church.

Towards the wedding of the Lamb

In the second part of the Book of Revelation (ch. 8–22), the action descends progressively from heaven to earth (cf. 8,5; 12,6; 14,16; 16,1; 21,2). The outlook is both more specific and more encompassing. More specific, because it is now a question of God's *judgment* working itself out in the course of history, in other words, the process by which the powers of evil are eliminated and the fullness of life bestowed upon the faithful who have been assailed by numerous trials. More encompassing, because the author of Revelation does not limit this judgment to a specific moment in time. Although for him it is basically identical with the death and resurrection of Christ, this act dilates until it fills the whole of human history and even beyond, for the roots of evil are pushed back to a time before the creation of humanity and attributed to "the great Dragon, the Serpent of old, the one called the Devil and Satan, the deceiver of the whole world" (12,9). The combat of evil against good fills time and space, causing an enormous amount of unhappiness and destruction. But God remains the Lord of history and, in the final analysis, the victories of evil are only apparent; they are, in fact, the progressive self-destruction of those who are destroying the earth (cf. 11,18). All this is recapitulated in the saving death of Christ, the event that marks the end of the old order and the advent of a new heaven and a new earth (cf. 21,1.5).

At the end of the book, all at once one image becomes central—that of the *woman*. The woman had played an important role at the beginning of the Book of Genesis, in the account of the origins of humankind (Eve). Afterwards her presence, although never vanishing completely, became more discreet. She reappeared particularly at critical moments of salvation history, for example on the threshold of the new covenant (Mary), or on Easter Sunday morning (Magdalen). And now, as our pilgrimage draws to an end, it is striking that the inspired writer once again gives a central place to the figure of the woman and reveals the fullness of her symbolic meaning.

We encounter this image first of all at the beginning of chapter 12:

> A great sign appeared in the sky: a Woman clothed with the sun, the moon under her feet, and on her head a crown of twelve stars. She was pregnant and cried out in the pain of childbirth ... The Woman gave birth to a male child, who is going to shepherd all the nations with a rod of iron ... (12,1–2.5a)

The Dragon chases her, and she flees into the desert, the traditional place of both refuge and trials (cf. PGod 35–42), where God protects her by means of a huge eagle and by saving her from the waters (12,4–6.13–17). These last elements are rather obvious allusions to the miracles of the Exodus (for the eagle cf. Ex 19,4; Deut 32,11), and so it seems clear that, rather than identifying this woman with a specific historical figure, we should see her as a symbol of God's partner in the drama of salvation history, of "humanity in its complex and troubled relationship with God."[4] At the time of the old economy, the woman corresponded essentially to the people of Israel, or else to the faithful remnant of that people. The prophets of old, incidentally, were not unaware of this correspondence, as shown by the oracles of Hosea concerning his unfaithful wife (Hos 1–3; PGod 70–72) and especially by the image of "Daughter Zion," where the capital of the nation, personified as a young woman, represents the faithful who are longing for their savior.[5]

This link between the image of the woman and the image of the city is reinforced by the next appearance of this symbol in the Book of Revelation. We meet the countertype of the first woman: a great Prostitute sitting on a beast, with the name "Babylon the Great" written on her forehead (Rev 17). The identification of idolatry, the refusal to serve the one true God, with prostitution also has a long history in Israel. Most commentators have seen the Prostitute as a symbol of imperial Rome, but recently the hypothesis has been put forward that she symbolizes the unfaithful Jerusalem, that is, the Jewish authorities who betrayed their God-given mission for their personal and collective profit.[6] We should not forget that diatribes against "unfaithful shepherds" were a commonplace of the preaching of the prophets of Israel. And elsewhere, Revelation speaks of "the great City, Sodom and Egypt as it is called symbolically, the place where their Lord also was crucified" (11,8). In any case, one thing is clear: the crucifixion of Jesus with the consent of the leaders of the people was the clearest manifestation of this possibility of turning the gift of a vocation into a personal privilege, the responsibility of accompanying others on their pilgrimage into a source of power and profit.

There is thus nothing mechanical about God's call. No one can absolve themselves from the need for *metanoia*, for a change of heart that must be accomplished over and over again. The Woman can always become the Prostitute; even Jerusalem can turn into Babylon and suffer her tragic fate. Chapter 18 of Revelation is a long lament of haunting beauty over the ruin of "the great City" because of her iniquities. But, perhaps as a means of discreetly informing us that destruction is not the essential aspect of divine judgment, immediately afterwards the positive side of the figure of the woman is brought to light:

There was a shout: "Hallelujah! For he has entered upon his reign, the Lord our God, the Almighty. Let us rejoice and be glad, and let us give glory to him, for the wedding of the Lamb has come, and his bride has made herself ready: linen garments, clean and bright, have been given her to wear" . . . Then he said to me: "Write: Happy those invited to the wedding feast of the Lamb!" (19,6b-9a)

"Babylon" disappears from the stage and is replaced by the "new Jerusalem" (21,2), the bride of the Lamb.

The dramatic movement of the Book of Revelation finally culminates in a marriage celebration, the wedding feast of the Lamb. After the disappearance of the powers of death, the Woman-City comes in her glory, or to put it another way, her true identity can finally appear. She can be seen for who she really is:

Then I saw a new heaven and a new earth—for the former heaven and the former earth went away, and there was no more sea. And I saw the Holy City, the new Jerusalem, coming down out of heaven, from God, made ready like a bride all adorned for her husband. And I heard a loud voice from the throne saying, "Look, here is the dwelling-place of God with human beings, and he will dwell with them, and they will be his people, and he will be God-with-them. He will wipe away every tear from their eyes, and there will be no more death. There will be no more weeping, crying or pain, because the old order of things has passed away." And the one sitting on the throne said, "Look, I am making all things new!" (21,1–5)

And the book concludes with a description of the Holy City, radiant with God's glory. The City has no Temple, since God is always with her in person, and no lamps, since "the glory of God illuminated her, and her lamp is the Lamb" (21,23). A river of water flows out from her, a wellspring of life for the inhabitants of the earth.

The Book of Revelation began with a glorious vision of the Son of Man (1,9–18) who is also the Lamb (5,6), and by the announcement of his coming (1,7). At the end of the book, we hear the announcement of the coming of the "wedding of the Lamb" (19,7) and the coming down from heaven of his bride, the Holy City (21,2). This is another extremely condensed way of summing up the entire history of salvation: by sending his Son, God prepares at the same time a partner capable of welcoming and loving him. Out of the human race which he created, God molds a "helpmate" worthy of himself. We must not forget that the Woman (12,1) and the Bride-City (21,2; 3,12) come down from *heaven*, in other words from God: any pretext for human beings to glorify themselves is thus definitively excluded. Their role is simply to "follow the Lamb wherever he goes" (14,4), and to "remain faithful till death" (2,10) to the gift they have received.

In spite of the customary reading, the images of the Book of Revelation do not only (or even primarily) describe a future reality. By the death and resurrection of Jesus Christ, the powers of evil have already been disarmed and banished; the universe has been renewed (21,5); the bride of the Lamb dressed for her wedding (19,7–8; cf. Ezek 16,8–14). From the Holy City, the community of believers, a spring of water gushes forth that is able to give, with no preconditions, the fullness of life to all who desire it (21,6; 22,1.17; cf. Ezek 47,1–12).

And yet, let us emphasize it one final time, this fulfillment already in progress does not diminish at all the desire and the dynamism of the participants in the drama. The closer it comes to the goal, the more intense the pilgrimage becomes. Instead of slowing down, it picks up speed. The urgency of the coming increases ("soon, quickly" 1,1; 22,6.7.20; "near" 1,3; 22,10; cf. also 2,16; 3,3.11.20; 10,6; 16,15). The presence of the Holy Spirit in our hearts, the perfect interiorization of the way of the Lord, is something that unsettles, a deepening of desire, a call to set out. That is the meaning of the cry with which the Book of Revelation, and thus the whole Bible, concludes. At this point there are only three actors: on the one hand the Spirit and redeemed humanity expressing a common longing, on the other the Bridegroom who is coming. Together they invite every human being to enter into this dynamic communion at the heart of the mystery of God:

Both the Spirit and the Bride say: Come! Let the one who hears say: Come! And let whoever is thirsty come, let whoever desires it take the water of life at no cost . . . Yes, I am coming quickly! (22,17.20)

And so that we do not remain outside, ashamed that we are not properly dressed (16,15; 22,14; cf. 7,14; Matt 22,11–13), so that we do not keep our doors closed (3,20), in our turn too we say: Maranatha! Yes, come, Lord Jesus!

Questions for Reflection

1. Every civilization has its values which either foster or inhibit the integral growth of human beings. In the society to which I belong, what are some of these values and their effects on me and on others?

2. In what way does the Judeo-Christian faith correspond to the basic makeup of the human being? What can the Church do to respond to the deepest thirsts of people, to speak their language?

3. Why does the author of the Book of Revelation describe Jesus as "a Lamb standing, as if slain" (Rev 5,6)? What is the significance of the image of the Lion applied to him (Rev 5,5; cf. Gen 49,9–10)? Why does the Lamb have seven horns and seven eyes (Rev 5,6; cf. Zech 4,10)?

4. What is the meaning of the figure of the Woman in Revelation? How does the image illuminate our vocation as believers? In what way does the figure of Mary, the mother of the Lord, help us to deepen this reflection? Why does the Bible close with the image of a marriage, of a wedding feast?

Notes

[1]For this kind of investigation that opens a great many perspectives, see the original and fascinating work of Eugenio Corsini, *The Apocalypse: The Perennial Revelation of Jesus Christ* (Wilmington, DE: Michael Glazier, Inc., 1983). The author breaks with the common interpretation that sees the Book of Revelation as essentially a prediction of the future and follows the more ancient commentators who viewed it as a meditation on the Hebrew Scriptures in the light of the death and resurrection of Christ. This interpretation has at least the great merit of making the unity of the book stand out more clearly, and provides a clarification of several details that have generally remained obscure.
[2]Cf. Corsini, pp. 61–66.
[3]See Chapter III, note 10.
[4]Corsini, p. 224. See also pp. 214–225.
[5]See Zeph 3,14–15; Zech 2,10; 9,9–10; Isa 12,6; 54,1; PGod 96–97,116, 178–179, 212. The image of the City (Jerusalem, Zion) as a personification of the people of the covenant is likewise deeply rooted in the Hebrew Scriptures. See PGod 124–127, 152–157, 194–199. Cf. also PGod 26 (n. 9), 79–83.
[6]Corsini, pp. 321–338. This interpretation, incidentally, provides an independent and unexpected confirmation of my investigation of the proto-apocalyptic literature in PGod 166–179.